The George Armstrong Story
Truth On The Ropes

The George Armstrong Story

Truth on the Ropes

George Armstrong

with

Evelyn Doody

OUT ON A LIMB

24 Old Gloucester Street
London WC1N 3XX

First Published in 1995
by
Out On A Limb Publishing
27 Old Gloucester Street,
London WC1N 3XX

Type-set in Times New Roman 10/15

THIS IS A TRUE STORY
THE NAMES OF MANY INDIVIDUALS HAVE BEEN
CHANGED

THOSE WHO SHOUT THE LOUDEST TO OBJECT TO
THIS BOOK
ARE THOSE WHO HAVE THE MOST TO HIDE

I THANK ALL THOSE WHO HAVE SUPPORTED ME
IN MY FIGHT
TO CLEAR MY NAME

A VERY SPECIAL THANK YOU TO
MR AND MRS BAILEY.
I AM ETERNALLY GRATEFUL

THANK YOU EVELYN FOR MAKING THIS BOOK A
REALITY

OUR COMBINED THANKS TO
ANNE
WHO HAS LOOKED AFTER US IN THE PRINCE OF
WALES

CONTENTS

INTRODUCTION

I MET George Armstrong after reading an advert he had placed in the *Southport Visiter* for someone to write his story.

We met in the *Prince of Wales* Hotel in Southport in November 1994. Since that time this has been our weekly office. We have shared coffee, biscuits, laughter and friendly disputes throughout our creation of this book. We have also become good pals.

When I first met George, I was impressed by his diamond white shirt, well pressed suit and immaculate appearance. He had the look and aura of a retired, well-to-do businessman. His white hair and good looks added the finishing touches to a distinguished looking man.

When he spoke, it was quickly. He told me his story in a tumble of words and often pulled out documents I was to read whilst he continued. As he talked I could see George was a desperate man and what he was telling me was incredible. This was a story I had not bargained for. It was a monster of a tale. I was hooked.

The story inspired me to write two songs for George: *My Fine Boys* and *In My Bingo Years*. We recorded them in April 1995. I sing, George narrates.

I have always believed in George; that is why I joined him in this fight for justice.

I could have written the book in the form of a biography but I felt I could convey his story better in the autobiographical first person. This after all is his story.

The cassette recording featuring *My Fine Boys* and *In My Bingo Years* can be obtained from:

OUT ON A LIMB PUBLISHING

27 Gloucester Street,

London WC1N 3XX.

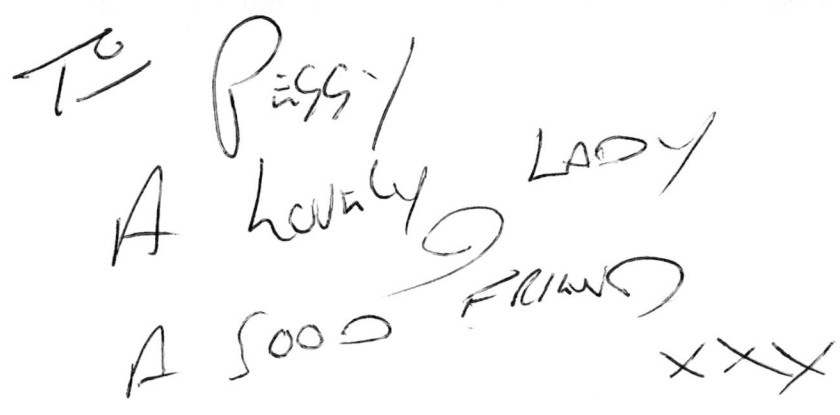

To Peggy
A Lovely Lady
A Good Friend xxx

DEDICATED TO

LEE

ALL MY FINE BOYS AND ALL MY FINE GIRLS

AND TO

LILLIAN

A FINE WIFE.

THANK YOU FOR LOVING ME

THANK YOU FOR KEEPING YOUR FAITH IN ME

Yours Sincerely

George Armstrong   May 1996

"I am ashamed the law is such an ass."
George Chapman c. 1559-1634
Revenge for Honour Act 3, Sc. 2

CHAPTER ONE
A PENNY FOR A SHIRT
TUPPENCE FOR A BLANKET

"**A** PENNY for a shirt and tuppence for a blanket" my mother would say as the door opened and cold suspicious eyes looked at her with uncertainty. Soon though, she would have them mirroring her smile and bringing out some work for her.

This was Liverpool in the early austere thirties. I was born on the 15th of March 1929; the place was my grandparents' tenement type house in Arlington street on Stanley Road, Kirkdale, almost facing where the new police station is today.

As soon as I could become of some help to our family income, I did my best to be a part of my mother's laundry service. I became the delivery boy. Times were desperate then, my mother used to walk all over the district knocking on doors and requesting "Washing and ironing please." She worked very, very hard, and our small back yard always seemed in full bloom of wet washing - even inside, dank clothing hung around like desolate children, sobbing, until my mother's busy hands made them ready for home.

These memories are from my second home in Back Castle Street, off Westminster Road. The front of the house was Boons Lino Shop which faced Everton Valley and the Lyric theatre.

From a window, we used to watch the annual parade marching towards the city, the star attraction the illuminated tram car. Many people would gather to see it, and it was always a popular occasion. Our house was 237 Westminster Road, near the Garrick Cinema, where Hollywood was yours for one penny admission. A treat to the flicks could set the imagination soaring for hours. Dreams and wonders could be discussed till bed time, when my father would open up the oven, take out bricks and wrap in an old cloth for us to take them to bed to keep warm.

My sister Gwen and I started our education at Westminster Road School. Our other grandmother, Mrs Hewitson, was the senior caretaker there and I was rather proud of that at the time. I made friends easily and one particular boy was a gypsy whose name was Dinky - he lived with his family in a caravan up an alley-way facing Brunswick Square. Next to the caravan was a building stabling five very sturdy horses owned by Mr Riley who ran a haulage business. I remember this place well, as it was near to the corner cake shop called Galley's where my mother used to send me for a pennyworth of stale cakes; Next door was Mrs Halliday's chip shop and I used to run errands for Mrs Halliday - my reward would be a penny worth of chips which I would share with Gwen.

My father was unemployed at the time, as were many men. But I remember he used to help a man who had a billiards room which had two tables. This too was on the Westminster Road, adjoining a corner shop called Ernie Jacksons where I used to have my father's battery accumulator charged for tuppence a time. Two old pennies could buy you quite a lot in those days. I think our rent was about five shillings a week, and because we were poor Gwen and I both went to Chalmers Hall for free school meals. The belly can't digest pride.

At the back of our house there was a large yard which housed a caravan where Mr Rigby lived with his dog. Eventually I was to make friends with him. I used to run errands, getting bread and other things for him. He used to make cans of soft soap and packets of soda which he would sell to other people. He also made clothes pegs, my mother being a ready customer.

Learning the work ethic, so early on in life, I soon supplemented my laundry delivery job with another from Cleggs Dairy in Goodhall Street. Yes, I delivered bottles of milk. I was also given transport, a bike with a square holder at the front. As this only held six bottles, my journeying to and from the dairy was frequent.

My mother, when she could, would take me and my sister Gwen shopping for what little she could afford. We would go down Great Homer Street which at that time boasted several butchers. Outside their shops, there stood tall barrels which contained various bits the butcher had not sold. Rich pickings for us poor folk and there were many like us. Stark and real poverty was a coat that clothed great numbers of my generation.

My mother, experienced in the mysteries of the barrel, would view the pigs feet, ribs and ox tail and buy the ingredients of our feast. She would then watch our tiny mouths water as she announced she would make us a pan of scouse when we got home. A happy heart is never poor, and we were loved. We knew our mum would cook us a meal fit for kings and in her court, we were her prince and princess.

On these outings grandmother and grandfather would sometimes come with us. Grandfather Armstrong would stop off at one of the many pubs in Great Homer Street to have a pint of brown ale. There he would sit happy and content amidst the wall to wall floor covering of sawdust, obscured only by the occasional, but necessary spittoon. In this harsh climate such pleasures were savoured. To keep warm, to eat, to live, people worked, and I think seeing my parents struggle to earn money to feed and clothe us, gave me a code of conduct for the future. My parents were industrious, and I think my success in the entertainment world stems from watching my parents use their skills and activities to provide for us. Both my parents were outgoing. They liked socialising too and they became keen dancers. Even in war time my mother managed to find time to dance, and she also won a few prizes too. Dad used to sing a little, so I probably inherited a little bit of showmanship from them.

3

In 1938 there was great excitement at the Armstrong house. We had a new baby brother. The name my parents had chosen for him was Lawrence and he brought much joy to my mother but within a few months, that joy was to turn to tears of sorrow, when my father broke the news he had been called up for army service. Now war talk whispered in all ears and the grown ups had more than poverty as their common enemy. We children understood little of what was going on, but then quite suddenly, the war came early to Gwen and me. It was late in August 1939, I remember my mother crying and taking us up to school. My sister and I had some clean clothes wrapped in paper tied with string. Parcels of small clothing and small children were gathered like lost mail. We were then walked in groups to Kirkdale station. We all crowded onto the platform and then climbed aboard the train, shuffling into coaches, some of us sure we would be home for tea, others excited finding the proceedings quite an adventure. As the train slowly drew away, mothers cried and waved, some holding children too young to leave. Our Lawrence cried too, nursed in mum's arms, his squeals fading as mum comforted him and wiped a quiet tear from her own eye. Our little hands signalled back our goodbye, as iron wheels moved the earth from all that was precious.

Evacuation to Winsford in Cheshire was not the end of the world, but by the time most of the children arrived there, it might just well have been. Firstly we were taken to the school hall and sat on benches and waited, the parcels now looking a bit dishevelled. Then, as if moving onto the sorting department, fifteen of us were taken outside and shunted on a bus. We arrived at a village called Meadow Bank near Whitegates in Cheshire. Now we found ourselves in a church hall and again we sat on benches and waited. Some of the parcels and the children were now looking ready to burst open. Bits of string twisted by worried fingers frayed under the strain. Tiny tears were swiftly wiped away in fear of fear. Throughout this time Gwen and I had held hands, jointly wrapped, which somehow made us feel stronger, but Gwen, sensing separation started to cry and said she wanted our mum. I gripped her hands, "Don't cry our sis, we'll soon be home" I comforted. But the parcels had not yet reached their destination. A lady walked up to us, undid the seal of our hands, and led me away. As I looked back I saw Gwen sobbing as another lady collected her.

But there is a happy ending, we were both very lucky with the wonderful people who looked after us throughout that time. When my brother Lawrence was old enough he came and lived with the family Gwen was staying with, and our mum did come and visit us over those next two years.

When I was thirteen, Gwen twelve and Lawrence four, my mother collected us and we returned home to Westminster Road. It had now been two years since the first bombs had fallen on Liverpool. The year was 1942, and air raids were still frequent. For us children, there was an air of excitement in having to run for cover to the public air raid shelters - ours was on the corner of Rummy Road. It was all so different from the quiet time we had spent in the country, but then no one thought the war would last so long. We were glad to be home again, back with our mum. Our education over that time was via a number of schools Westminster Road, Lambeth Road and Priory Road. In my final year, I became involved with the senior football team - our trainer was a Mr Jones. We must have not been too bad as we did play in the school finals held at Everton Football club. These were happy escapist hours, when the day to day struggle of war time was ever present. The city appeared half eaten, as though some cruel iron giant had come by night and devoured it. Daylight reality was relying on ration books and making do. These were strange and frightening times. Air raid sirens wailed, the skies flashed with dark colours and bunches of sudden stars. Then there would come the quiet, as black smoke, like tired ghosts appeared from the debris. The city quaked but its people were silent and forbearing, there was a strength amongst us people that bound us together like one sad family.

I was fourteen now, and wanted to play a man's part in the world, so it was time to leave my school days behind. By now my mother Lillian had taken a job in a munitions factory in Longmoor, and our next door neighbour, Mrs Dean, looked after Gwen and Lawrence. I knew I was a growing lad, needing more food and that was still scarce, unless you could pay black market prices. We did however have a little good fortune in that area - our uncle Nelson who lived in Smeaton street was a pigeon fancier. Now and then he would provide pigeons for us; my mother was very grateful for these and so were we.

There seemed to be more real charity about then. People would share what they had. I knew then that I must do my bit. I had to earn a mans wage. The war made you grow up fast. Life and death stalked on every corner and it was round about this time that a bomb fell on Ruskin Street killing and injuring several people. Things like that happening made you feel you wanted to fight back, but always the real fight was keeping alive and helping one another. Determined I would get into uniform, I managed to join the Army cadets. I confess I lied about my age, but a lot of lads did. Getting into uniform made you feel you were a part of it, fighting the war. In reality our service was confined to drilling. Meantime I had also acquired my first job with Burton's Barges. Our job was to unload the brown sugar on to the barges, after which we would be towed in line up the River Mersey with other barges, and then via canals near Warrington until we reached the Sankey Sugar works. It was whilst doing this work I was offered another job. We had been moving sugar off a ship called the *Anglian Coast*, and part of my job was to go aboard to make cans of tea for the dockers. I was chatting to the cook when he suddenly said "Do you want a job?". I looked at him and nodded, then said yes. I remember he glanced at me a couple of times and asked, "How old are you?"

"Fifteen and a half" I quickly answered, knowing full well you had to be this age by law to obtain work.

"If you can get your cards and identity card, you can start to-morrow," he told me. I knew I couldn't possibly miss this chance to better myself and help my family.

Spurred on by impetuous youth, I managed to jump on the overhead train, and got my cards from Burton's Barges offices. Then rushed over to the post office in Victoria Street. There I changed my date of birth by changing the 1929 to 1928, thus giving me an eligible age to take the job on the ship. I then called to see a Mr Miller with whom I had made friends at the Merchant Navy Pool at Corn Hill. I had fetched tea and collected a paper for him many times. Now he assisted me with sorting out my papers and arranging my photograph to be taken.

When I arrived home, there was no-one in. My mother was now a clippie, a conductress on the trams and worked shifts. Gwen and Lawrence were at school. I gathered my clothes in a large sack, then wrote a letter to mum saying I would be away for a few days. My work had involved staying away some nights, so I was hoping the news of my new job with a coaster ship would not upset her too much. I said we would be going to Swansea, Cardiff and Preston and that I might even be gone about two weeks. I packed my mother's gas mask and tin hat. Being only fourteen I thought these things would be of more use to me going to sea than to my mother touring Liverpool on a tram. My mother was employed by Liverpool Corporation Passenger Transport Department, and so naturally painted on the tin hat was L.C.P.T. which was going to look rather odd once aboard ship. Still in my excitement I packed them away quite sure I needed them. I left my little note on the table and looked back at it as I closed the door. I hoped my mother wouldn't be too upset that I had run off to sea like this. I would be home soon enough, and this time with better pay. I closed the door and went on my way. As I jumped on the 61 bus to Gladstone Dock, I felt assured and in control of my life. I was fourteen years old, a child desperate to be part of that wider world. By the time I was on the overhead train to Huskisson Dock, the bravado of adventure had faded a little as the child in the man came face to face with his ship of dreams.

Once on board ship, the cook showed me to a very small cabin situated at the stern of the ship. After that I went up to the deck and met two Royal Navy sailors. I was told they had been attached to the *Anglian Coast* and that they were D.E.M.'s gunners who would man and fire the two Lewis guns which were situated right above my cabin.

So there I was, at last at sea, on a real ship with guns, any young boys dream come true - well not quite. I was back home in a couple of weeks and able to give my mother a little more of my earnings. She still wasn't too happy with my new occupation but I knew she would come round in the end.

After a few months coasting I decided I wanted to try a deep sea ship and this led me to the Fred Olsen line. I was given the post of *Messen Gut* - in English, Mess Boy. The ship was the *Abraham Lincoln* and the ratings were all Norwegian but one or two of the crew were English.

At this point I had no idea where we were bound and so it came as a wonderful surprise when I was told we would be sailing to New York. I confess my sea legs were still a little wobbly, and it would take some time before I overcame sea sickness.

'New York, New York. So good they named it twice' - and what a place it was! My eyes must have been like dinner plates but so were those of the New Yorkers' when they saw the Norwegian sailors. You see, their uniforms were almost exactly the same design as those worn by the German navy. People were always taking a second look.

So there I was, George Armstrong only fourteen seeing the sights of New York. The little lad who used to deliver washing for his mam, there in America.

Our first call was to 42nd Street, and The Stage Door canteen which had become a meeting place for service men. Someone in there actually gave us tickets to see Frank Sinatra at the Roxy. Excited and eager to see a real star, we made our way to Times Square, but so it seems had several hundred other fans. We queued for several hours trying to get in, but sad to say the queues of people waiting were endless. We just never had the time. But we did get to see the Statue of Liberty, the wonderful view of Coney Island and eat at the Automat in Times Square. The Automat was incredible, well ahead of its time. You could walk in, place your money in a machine and have your meal in seconds. You just picked the meal you wanted, pressed a button, and out it popped.

It was in New York I also acquired my tattoo. Being the youngest of the bunch I went around with, I didn't always latch on to all the antics the lads got up to. In those days some of the drug stores had drinking parlours in the rear of their premises. There would also be ladies available for those seeking a little more than a quiet drink. On one particular occasion, there was a tattoo artist right next door to a drug store where some of the lads were eyeing the ladies and having a couple of drinks. A couple went in and I stood by watching. The tattooist seeing I was much younger suddenly called me over and said, "Come here son, lets give you a special memory of New York". I still have the tattoo; it says simply, 'New York 1943'.

The *Queen Mary* lay berthed near to our ship, her role at that time being to ship out American troops to England.

During my voyages aboard the *Abraham Lincoln* we experienced U- boat alarms at night, and also endured air attacks. These were all very frightening. Our ship was a motor vessel and was capable of reaching eighteen knots. She was also chosen as the commodore ship of several convoys which she would control. In a convoy there could be 80 to 100 ships at any one time and during these trips several ships would be lost despite the tremendous courage and strength of our Navy.

At the rear of the convoy would sail small ships known as Q-boats which would pick up survivors of any sunken vessels, no other vessel being allowed to pick up personnel. They had to drift to the rear of the convoy to survive.

By now my mother had accepted my career as a seaman. My father had also been home on leave from the army several times and had given his approval. It probably helped all round that I was sending money home. My pay was nine pounds a week, and I sent my mother two. Furthermore I wasn't there to eat her out of house and home. I was also being paid a further seven pounds a month danger money, as were all seaman at this time.

Eventually though I would have to sail home, and it was illness that took me back. Whilst on a trip to West Africa, I developed an infection in my hand - it was quite bad and I ended up in a hospital in Lagos where I remained for six days before returning home. If you are at sea several months you were entitled to request shore leave, and so since I was still weak from my illness, I took a couple of months leave. I have fond memories of my visits on that leave to *The Seven Steps* pub near Harrington Dock, Toxteth. This pub had a wonderful atmosphere and had been a place to gather throughout the war years.

But I couldn't rest for long. I obtained a temporary job in the Tillosons Paper factory on Commercial Road. My role there was that of an Ink Spot, no not singing. I had to fill the machines with coloured ink. The machines would then print the wording on the cigarette packets. It was also on this shore leave that I took up an interest in boxing and joined the Star Boxing club on the corner of Taylor Street and Great Homer Street. I'll tell you more about that later.

After those very different few weeks, I was back to sea sailing with *The New Zealand Star* - a lovely vessel, with a rake funnel and only one mast forward. It took only thirty two passengers and boasted R.D.F (Radio Location Finder, more commonly referred to as Radar) - one of the first ships to have it on board. It was sited behind the bridge alongside a heavy six inch gun. On the bow was sited two 25lb guns, and a six inch at the rear. I was very proud to be on this ship which looked every inch of an armed cruiser in her smart battleship grey.

My part in this Iron Lady was to peel spuds, help prepare food and wash pans. I must have peeled thousands of potatoes on the voyage.

Sailing to Buenos Aires, South America and Montevideo to pick up a cargo of meat, our beautiful grey lady suddenly came under attack. I was collecting a bag of potatoes from the locker situated on the boat deck, when one of the gunners pointed to a smudge of smoke on the horizon. He told me we were on alert as German raiders were still active.

Our attacker was to fire four shots across our bows, instructing the ship to heave to. Luckily our Captain was the very respected Captain McFarland, his control of this situation being to ensure the safety of all our lives. All ships of course were committed to radio silence, throughout this time, and so contact was made by lamp and codes. In this case, the unidentified ship turned out to be a Free French cruiser, so once this awkward situation had been resolved, Captain McFarland moved us onwards to our destination. Our Captain, no stranger to steel nerve, was the same McFarland that had earlier on in his career, guided a convoy of twenty five ships, all that was left from the terrible devastation of air and U- boat attacks, into the bay of Malta. In fact, it is said McFarland's efforts, along with his crew's, played a vital role in saving Malta from invasion. We were in a time of history making, and sailing with the history makers.

On our arrival in Montevideo, I witnessed the wreckage of the infamous German battleship the the *Admiral Graf Spee*, which had by now become a part of history. Ashore, several of us were taken on what can only be described as a tour. It was of course still neutral there. In fact there was a German embassy with two German guards directly placed outside its entrance. But the most poignant was the visit to the grave of Hans Langsdorff, the Captain of the *Admiral Graf Spee*. This pocket battleship, sank nine ships before she came to her sad end. The ship had spent four days in Montevideo for repairs, whilst two of our cruisers, the *Ajax* and the *Achilles*, waited for her return to battle. The cruisers needed reinforcements and called up the *Cumberland*. The *Graf Spee* would have met defeat and knowing this, the crew took her a little way out of the harbour and scuttled her to prevent our ships from taking her.

Three days later, the Captain shot himself, rather than face the personal disgrace to his honour. Nearby were the graves of other naval ratings who had also lost their lives in this tragic conflict that was to be known as THE BATTLE FOR THE RIVER PLATE.

So this was the grown up world I had longed to be a part of, and this was my enemy. I couldn't help but feel the futility of it, a sadness. A battle had been won there, but twisted iron and a handful of graves that held other mother's sons were all that could be counted. I knew I had much to learn about life.

It was whilst I was visiting South American ports that I started taking boxing seriously. Maybe it was a way to let off steam but either way I enjoyed it. My father had been a well known amateur boxer before I was born, so I was just taking over where Dad had left off. I came up against a local boy there and did well. Following this I took on other fights, and when I was home in Liverpool, I trained at the Star Boxing club. There were some up-and-coming boys there at the time: Al Hutt, Eric Riley and a future British English champion Stan Rowan. So I was in good company. The training and advice I was given was worth its weight in gold. Later I was to be successful against the Lancashire area champion - the prize oddly enough was a tea service which my mother kept for many years.

When the war years were behind me, like so many, I was uncertain where life would take me. There was talk of a new order, things were going to change. On a day to day basis this was hard to appreciate. You still needed your daily bread while you waited for jam tomorrow. I suppose I was lucky, I still had the sea to sail my dreams upon, and by now I had sailed on many ships. Some of my dreams of youth had been fulfilled, but there were still many more in the hold.

In February 1947 I was a month away from my eighteenth birthday. My ship at this time was the *Herdsman*. We were heading for South Africa, calling at Cape Town, Durban and Port Elizabeth. There had been much talk of the Royal visit to South Africa,

King George VI and the Queen Elizabeth were heading there too. Their ship being the *H.M.S Vanguard*. So when we found ourselves berthed next to the battleship *H.M.S Vanguard* it was not at all surprising we chatted to her crew. These discussions, I confess, ran along usual lines, the punch line always ending with "Where can you get a drink"? Someone always knew. Another predictable situation was that we on the *Herdsman* were running short of money by then. We had been there about ten days and most of us had spent money on presents for home or squandered it, usually a bit of both. But then suddenly I was sure good fortune had smiled on me. As it was, I think Lady Luck may have been out the port hole. The Chief steward had called me on one side and asked me to dispose of some damaged drums of liquid, soft soap. The lads and I chatted and one of them asked the South African security chap if he or his friend would like to buy it. Next thing we knew, he had arranged his friend who had a dockside café to buy it off us.

Money in the pocket, brains left at home, we eagerly went ashore to spend it. There was a very celebratory air about the place due to the Royal couple being there, and whilst we were enjoying ourselves at a local Hotel, some dignitaries asked us to join with them in celebrating the visit of our King and Queen. Why not, we thought? The atmosphere was almost carnival, and as a group of mixed crew members, some from the *Herdsman* some from the *Vanguard*, we certainly had a merry time. They treated us like V.I.P's and it was quite clear they thought we were all *H.M.S Vanguard* crew members. This was an easy mistake to make, as we were all in tropical dress uniform. But the party always ends, and this one was also to end my sea faring days for good.

At nine o' clock next morning the *Herdsman* left port and sailed without five crew members. Sadly I was one of them. How we managed to miss our ship is still a mystery to me. But then so is most of the later part of that extraordinary twenty four hours. All that was left behind were our clothes and belongings. We had not been there for our ship, and in return our ship was not going to be there for us. It took three days and two nights by train to rejoin our ship. All other transport being unavailable due to the Royal visit. When we did arrive in Cape Town we were held in an immigration centre for six days awaiting the arrival of our Ship, which was still voyaging around the South African coast. When she did arrive, our Captain severely reprimanded us and made it clear we would be reported to the Seaman's Pool on our arrival back in England. We knew this was a serious matter, so we were dejected and full of remorse but the rules had been broken and we had to face the consequenses.

So it came to pass, by way of punishment, that I was drafted into the army, this being the result of my misdemeanour. The months passed and soon I was nineteen, and compelled to serve my twelve months National Service. I was first based at the Army Barracks at High Leigh in Warrington. Then, after ten weeks of basic training, I was posted to the Royal Artillery Camp at Tonfanau, North Wales. I found I loved the army and signed on for five years with the colours and seven in the reserves, in the Royal Artillery.

When I first went on parade with the army, I used to get an awful lot of stick from the lads. I was duty bound to wear my campaign medals. As I was only nineteen remember, and the lads wouldn't believe I had earned them. I tried avoiding wearing them, but I was told off in no uncertain terms about this and was forced to obey. One was the North African Ribbon, the other the Atlantic Star, this being for six months' deep sea service between 1939 and 1943. Also I had the Victory medal. The lads thought I was just swanking; they felt I was too young to have earned these medals, but of course I had gone to sea as a very young lad after lying about my age. Eventually, when they got to know me they did come to believe me.

Two important things happened at Tonfanau. Firstly I realised I could organise people, and my interest in sport led me to the post of permanent physical staff training instructor. It was also at this time that boxing featured once again in my life, when I became a member of the Regimental Boxing Team. My boxing weight at the time was lightweight, but eventually went up to welterweight. This was highly successful for me and I became Regional Area Boxing Champion.

The other thing that happened was falling in love. I met a young Welsh girl who was a member of the N.A.F.F.I. She was one of the staff who provided catering services and other facilities to the camp. There were about two thousand men of all ranks and regiments stationed there at the time.

Needless to say we were very young and I fell very much in love. Its not easy to say this, but the girl became pregnant. There was no problem with this as far as I could see. I wanted to marry her, but it was not to be. I visited her parents in Cardiff to talk of marriage, but was devastated to find out she was already married. On my return to barracks I received a letter from her saying she was going to stay with her parents and have the baby adopted. I was very hurt by this and found myself broken by the affair. She later wrote and told me she had given birth to a little boy whom she had named George. Sad to say, the little boy was adopted and that period of my life still chills my heart.

It was not surprising I requested a posting around this time. My senior instructor thankfully was sympathetic and supported my application. Firstly though, I was assigned to Oswestry, where I went through their advanced physical training course. It was there I was made Bombardier, a rank which held two stripes above the crossed swords of the Physical Training Regiment. When I had completed my training, I was posted to The Royal Artillery Depôt in Woolwich for a short time, this prior to being sent out to the Middle East.

****

Top: A copy of the cassette recording that was played at my two trials.

Below: Me with my regulation-issue plastic bag.

CHAPTER TWO
BROKEN HEARTS - BOXING - BINGO

P ARADE in the Middle East was at six in the morning. So there was time in the latter part of the day for sports. Football, cricket and badminton were very popular with the lads. I once played against David Hickson who later was to become a famous Everton player.

The service and sport were all very stimulating for me, but I did miss the lack of female company. Women were very much a minority group in Egypt; there were fifteen to twenty thousand service men and only approximately two thousand women, these being made up from the Womens Air Force Regiment and the Womens Army Training Regiment.

Fortunately for me, I was chosen to referee WAFFS and ATS netball and basketball games. This brought with it a few headaches, but it was a pleasant change from constant male company. On a personal level I was lucky to make friends with a very nice person by the name of Joyce, but all too soon the friendship became a love affair, and once again I found I had made the girl pregnant. Joyce was swiftly returned to England to await the birth of our child, which was a little girl. I was the next one sent home, this time to Aldershot, where I was put through another Physical Training course. Whilst in Aldershot I was called to a hearing in Truro to confirm I was the father of the child Joyce had given birth to. I was then instructed to pay about seven and six in maintenance until the child was fourteen. I did this willingly. My only regret is to have missed out on seeing these children grow. As it was, Joyce had also found a new gentleman friend, and so I was ill fated with both love affairs. All I know now, is that I have two children I would dearly love to see before I die, but I know that is very much a dream.

After my two disasters in love, I was in no hurry to have my heart broken again, and so I gave my energy to boxing. I boxed in Aldershot and Liverpool, where I had started taking home leave. On a few occasions there I met up with a lovely young lady called Lillian. We dated, but I was still keeping my eye fixed on my boxing interests. Boxing was something I had control over, and it was proving good for my self-esteem. It was whilst I was stationed at Aldershot that a man from Jack Solomon's Gym approached me and invited me down to Windmill Street in London to meet the great man himself. I also met Freddie Mills and his manager Ted Broadribb. I felt so good being in the company of such well known professional people. I was after all only at amateur status and they needn't have given me their valuable time. I couldn't believe it when Freddie and Ted watched me go three rounds with a professional boxer, an honour indeed. But there was more to come. Later over a coffee Ted asked if I could obtain my release from the army. He said he would like to take me on if I would turn professional and stay under his guidance. It was like a dream come true. I answered yes to everything he said and I must have grinned like a Cheshire cat. Next day I attended the gym in Windmill street and did some practice there. Afterwards I was fortunate to be taken across to the then famous Windmill theatre. I could hardly believe my eyes when I was introduced to Terry Thomas who was there with a group of friends. Terry was such a nice chap and I had a marvellous evening in the company of Freddie and Terry, who in their very different ways, proved wonderfully entertaining people. That night I felt sure my life was going to change dramatically. I also realised I had a bit of the showman in me. I didn't mind an audience. As an instructor I had an audience; it was the same as a boxer. My mind was full of better things to come, and I couldn't wait to get home and tell Lillian, who by now seemed to be taking up more of my thoughts than I had intended.

I was riding high that night, but it turned out that I was riding for a fall. My discharge from the army hit a snag, and I was still duty bound to complete my posting in Egypt. There seemed no way around it. I was obviously not destined to become a professional boxer. In the meantime I did manage to box against the American army several times, and I also managed to box in the Albert Hall in London, but I slowly accepted this was not where the fates were leading me.

When I had completed my stint in the Middle East, I was returned to Woolwich, England to await my demob. I have mixed memories of that last posting. I had returned a qualified Physical Training Instructor, but my thoughts were still what might have been if I could have been bought out of the army. But these personal plans seemed dwarfed alongside the political climate that had evolved out there. In 1952 King Farouk abdicated causing untold unrest and many problems for those stationed out there.

But the winds of change were blowing in the world, and it was time for me to make changes.

On my return to Liverpool, I lived with my mother, and brother Lawrence in Westminster Road - no great changes there, but that was comforting. My sister Gwen I remember was full of a job she had applied for, based in the Isle of Man, and so it didn't seem five minutes before she was off to make her fortune there. My itchy feet now sought some kind of substance. I wanted to make something of my life, and that life needed a partner. The lovely Lillian, I mentioned earlier, now started to play a much greater role in my future. We were in love, we planned to marry, but I am ashamed to say we didn't marry until she had given birth to our beautiful daughter Sandra Lillian. Our marriage took place in the Church of St Christopher, in Lorenzo Drive, Liverpool, in 1951. We were poor, but we had the future before us and a lovely little girl. What I needed now was a good job with good pay. I knew that was the same dream as several other million men, and I soon discovered the qualifications I had attained in the army were going to be of little use in civvy street, but these were early days and the experience of my service days would eventually pay off.

The position I had now was in a Bakery, putting lids on pies then egg whiting them. I was part of the assembly line before the pies were pushed into large ovens - automation was purely physical in our Bakery.

From there, I moved on the Vernons Industry where I was employed as a normaliser, a rather fancy name for lowering and dipping control panels for aircraft in liquid that would strengthen and reinforce their quality.

Next came the chance of a two pound a week increase working for the Co-op Bakery Department on Walton Road. My title now was co driver, the vehicle being horse drawn. The horse knew the round better than anyone, and more times than not I had to ride shot gun, sitting at the back to stop the kids from jumping on for a free ride. I was with that company quite a few months, eventually having my own horse and vehicle. I became quite fond of that old horse, but I needed more money. We had two children now, our second child being a boy we had named Lawrence. We also had acquired a flat in Kirkby which we had obtained with the help of Bessie Braddock, the Labour M.P. for our district. What a marvellous person she was. Until that time we had lived with Mum in Westminster Road, but the time had come to make our own home. It was now 1953 and my employment had changed to erecting television aerials for Stuart and Dorfman, the owner being a very generous man by the name of Benny Dorfman. It was hard going but the pay was ten pounds a week plus two shillings bonus after the first ten aerials erected. This was really demanding work - those tenement buildings were high - but my endurance training, strength and youth kept me going. My mate, who worked alongside me in this job was a chap by the name of Ray Ennis. Several years later,

Ray was to become one of the Swinging Blue Jeans, a famous Mersey group whose record, The Hippy Hippy Shake, stayed at Number Two in the charts for seventeen weeks, but that was to be ten years later. In those days the last thing we needed was the shakes.

Whilst working as a rigger, I found a house I liked for us in Roby. It was a new house and I needed a hundred pounds deposit. I casually mentioned this to Mr Benny Dorfman's brother and to my surprise Benny sent for me, and said he was pleased with my work and would be happy to introduce me to his bank. I was over the moon and eternally grateful to that man as it was a wonderful opportunity to become an independent home-owner. Our near neighbours by the way were Herman, of Herman and the Hermits fame, also Billy Foulkes, Captain of the famous Matt Busby football team.

Eventually I did move on from Mr Dorfman's employ. I left with his recommendation gladly given. This time I was Area Supervisor with Austin Fenwick. Austin was a personal friend of John Bloom, a self made millionaire. Both had been in the RAF together and hit upon the idea of importing washing machines at low cost and then retailing them out at a profit. This proved successful, John Bloom eventually going to America to even greater success and wealth.

I got this job because Mr Fenwick was impressed with my service record and could see that I had been in charge of men in my role as a training officer. From area supervisor, I eventually became a manager controlling twelve salesmen. My position was a responsible one. I had to collate records and handle large amounts of money which I would hand-deliver every week to the head office in Stoke on Trent. In the meantime my family had settled into our new home and things were moving in the right direction.

On one occasion when I was out chasing a bad payment, I was sitting in my car outside the Locarno ballroom on West Derby Road. I had fond memories of the place as it was there that I had met my wife Lil. I was unsure of the best way to a particular road, and so called over the man who had stepped out of the building. The name of the man was John Morgan He told me he was the box office manager, and he suggested I go inside for a coffee whilst he looked up the best access to the road I wanted. Little did I realise that this meeting was to change my whole career and lifestyle. This was to be the beginning of a wonderful part of my life; I was about to embark on a journey many men can only dream of. Over that cup of coffee John told me he was looking for a part-time doorman and supervisor; the hours were 7.15 p.m. until 12.30 a.m. The wage? That was seven and six pence. John told me that if I could get hold of a bow tie and turn up at seven thirty, the job was mine. I was there on the dot. So was my bow tie!

I managed both day and night jobs quite well for a time. Also Lil had now acquired a position as a typist for the English Electric Company in Liverpool. So things were financially much better for us. Our family was growing too - we had another little girl we called Patsy, then came Gary.

When John Morgan told me he was being moved to the Grafton Ballroom next door to the Locarno, he asked me to join him there as full-time box office manager. I was thrilled. I had really taken to the Mecca way of doing things and in my mind I set myself a target. I would be a manager within twelve months. My enthusiasm was greatly inspired by those I was to be working with. John's boss at the Grafton was to be Tom Reid, one of Mecca's most senior managers. As I was working alongside very professional people, it was inevitable that I would learn from them.

After talking things over with Lil, I told John I would be delighted to join him. Now I was full time with Mecca and what a wonderful experience that was going to be. I cannot stress enough my admiration for the Mecca Empire and what it gave to me. Yes, I gave too. I worked hard, played hard and became a success within the company, but it was a business love affair, and I enjoyed every second of it.

To become a Mecca manager was not an easy task, the Company set the highest possible standard for their managers and once they were in a position of authority they seldom moved on. They moved sideways, across, up and down but hardly ever did they move out. But now greater opportunity was to knock in the shape of a new venture called BINGO. Eric Morley had originated BINGO, from an idea he had come across in the U.S.A. Eric could possibly foresee that the market trend would move away from live music. In addition the cinemas and theatres that had once been so popular were now on the decline - both would eventually prove ideal prime Bingo venues. The future wanted new entertainment. It was after all 1958 and there was room for new ideas. At first Bingo was restricted to Saturday and Sunday afternoons, a small beginning for what was to become a multi-million pound business that would turn the whole of the UK BINGO CRAZY.

It was at this time that Eric put it out amongst his staff that he wanted managers for this new business, the Bingo business. I knew this was my chance to move up in the Mecca Empire, so on the recommendation of my manager at that time, Mr Reid, I was made trainee manager at the Derby Hippodrome. Within eight months I was manager, I had also developed a little of my showmanship skills, and was bringing in good profits for the Hippodrome. At the time we had people in like Noel Gordon of Lunch Box and Crossroads fame, there was also a marvellously successful show featuring Frankie Vaughan and another hilarious time we had, the late Arthur Haines.

But my Mecca career wasn't all Bingo, not at all. I was also to become Box office manager of the Locarno and Grafton Ballroom in West Derby road. All these detours giving me good employment and added business training for the future. It was whilst working at the Locarno West Derby Road that I first met the Beatles, we booked them there. Music was still very much live in the ballrooms, but the groups had started a new trend. A trend which would eventually move out the big bands the Locarno scene was so famous for.

23

I obtained Paul McCartney's autograph many times because he used to have to sign the docket for the money the group were paid. It seems crazy now, but we paid them £12 for two half hour spots. I'm sure the boys were glad of it too in those early days. But I was to meet the Beatles on many more occasions. I was at the Liverpool Locarno when 'Ferry Across the Mersey' was being made. I also had the privilege of meeting several people involved with the film, including Gerry and the Pacemakers. On another occasion the Beatles were playing York Rialto, where the manager was Don Mc-Callion, a good pal of mine, later to become Eric Morley's right hand man. We had to smuggle them in because the crowds were unbelievable. The lads stayed at the Railway Inn, - which had been kept very hush-hush so they could retire early.

Another time at the Locarno West Derby Road, I met Brian Epstein, Bob Wooler, the Cavern DJ and Allan Williams who was the Beatles first manager. Bob and Allan were to become good friends of mine. But let's just go back to Mecca managers for a moment. You may be surprised to discover that performer and pro-moter Larry Page of the now famous Page One Records had been honoured with the title of Mecca manager, and so had DJ, fund raiser JIM'LL FIX IT, now Sir Jimmy Saville. Mecca proving a good grounding base for their future success.

I know I go on about this, but I can't stress enough my apprecia-tion for this company. Eric Morley was a tough man, but fair. If you got it wrong you would be on the train down to see him in person. He never minced words, but on the other hand, if you did well he would lavish praise upon you.

I had a wonderful time with Mecca. I have great respect for the people I worked alongside, those I worked for and the people who worked for the organisation. I also managed to hear some good music too - Mecca bands that were to become household names. I'm sure everyone has heard of Ray MacVay and Tony Evans; if not, they have missed some fine music. Then there were the stars, the genius comedy of Ken Dodd, who actually did me the honour of joining me for a drink in my office. I became good friends with

Doddy. The personalities like Diddy David Hamilton, so named by Doddy, Tony Holland the muscle man, who became another friend. Jimmy Tarbuck, Bob Hope, the names are endless. From doorman to winner of the best best showman of the year and the best business. Okay, I may be blowing my trumpet here, but I'm proud of what I achieved, and I hope it will go some of the way in showing you what kind of man I am.

It was in 1961 that I came into contact with Bob Hope. At the time I was assisting with the Miss World contest. Bob was on the panel of judges, but to be fair, I think in those days my eyes were firmly set on the contestants. What gorgeous girls they were!

Around this time I became rather close to a lady called Diana Westbury who went on to become Miss World. Another lady contestant of that era was Rosemary Franklin - now a well-known personality in one of the Australian soaps. These were heady days and I was a successful young man. Being amongst these beautiful woman was a temptation to any man, and any red-blooded male would have felt special to be around these woman.

Then there was the Ghost I met. Well we were more like passing ships in the night, and to be frank at the time I was unaware of a ghostly presence. The place was the Derby Hippodrome, my role there was the manager. When I first went to Derby Hippodrome, I used to sleep in the building seven nights a week. My home was still in Huyton, and it was too far to travel to and fro to Liverpool. I was eventually to move there, but until that time I would use a camp bed and stay every night in the theatre. In the main I would use the office, but it had a sloping floor and I suffered quite a lot at the time from headaches. I thought it may have been due to the floor level, but in truth it was probably due to long hours, pressure of work, and not eating right. Today they would call it executive stress.

One night after three beers at the local pub near the theatre, I came back and sat and chatted with the night watchman, and then decided to carry my bed up to one of the dressing rooms. There were three dressing rooms, numbered One,Two and Three. All were very much alike, and so I don't know what compelled me to climb three flights of iron staircase and choose dressing room Number Two. Once inside I set up my bed, lay down and covered myself. Sleep soon came. I have no idea what time it was, but I was roused in a half sleep to hear footsteps, and someone trying the door to dressing room Number One. Then footsteps again. Tired and aware the night watchman was in, I turned over and waited for sleep. Suddenly my bedclothes were pulled back. I shivered and, half awake, looked about me, but there was no one there. I pulled the bedclothes over me again and once more tried for sleep. Again the bedclothes peeled back leaving me uncovered. I was too tired to care who it was, and my mind seemed to dismiss the fact that there had been no-one present to pull back the bedclothes. I blinked, pulled up the covers and turned over and lay in a half sleep. The footsteps then could be heard again, this time it seemed they were heading for the roofspace. Exhausted from a long day, I ignored the intruder, confident our night watchman would deal with him.

Next morning whilst having a coffee with my secretary Jill, I happened to mention my strange night in dressing room Two.

"It's the theatre ghost George" she told me.

I laughed. "You're joking" I answered.

She smiled and shook her head, then went on to explain the ghost had been with the theatre a long time. In future I made a point of avoiding those old dressing rooms and put up with the sloping floor of the office until I arranged other sleeping arrangements.

These arrangements eventually meant a house move for the family. It was a growing family too as I once again became a proud father. We had a little boy, we called that particular bundle of mischief Carl.

As my distinction with Mecca grew from strength to strength, I eventually reached the envied position as a trouble-shooter - a role involving complex, management skills which were tested to the limit, and marketing and promotive capabilities which were firmly backed up with hands-on application. A trouble shooter would be sent into a venue if the takings on that hall had considerably fallen for two or more nights. To put it bluntly, lost profits. Our role was to go in and find out what had gone wrong, and then help guide the manager into a more profitable approach. This could mean organizing promotions, special offers and events. It was a demanding job, but I enjoyed the diversity. In fact I thrived on it and found the change very rewarding. But time was moving on, and my wife was tired of moving around and furthermore I was working away from home quite often in my role as trouble shooter. I knew one day I would have to carve a new direction for myself.

The culmination of my Mecca years has to be 1962, when I managed to win the exclusive Gold Cup, which was presented to me by Carl Hieman at the Empire Ballroom in Leicester Square, London. I beat ninety two Mecca venues and became best showman of the year and also won the Best Business Award. As if this wasn't enough, I was also presented with a new car, the new Hillman Imp. I was very well aware I hadn't reached that point on my own as I had had tremendous support from the staff I worked with. I had been given encouragement and advice from Head Office and my managing colleagues. But I can't deny how proud I was to be so successful and stand there shaking the hand of Mr Mecca himself, Carl Hieman.

It was in these jubilant times that Mark came on the scene. A beautiful little boy, a joy to us all. A new birth, and new ideas were sweeping me along and I was on top of the world. By now, Lil and I had produced six healthy and happy children. The jewels in the crown of my success.

When I eventually left Mecca, I had served them well for sixteen years. My departure had developed from a disagreement with a district manager who was managing the Pavilion Theatre at the time. It was on a matter of policy that we came to grief, but that is history now and best left to the past. Times and people change. I knew the time had come for me to move along in life.

Sydney Lever was a prominent entrepreneur on Merseyside whon I met him, with several clubs in the area, one of them being Tito's night club. Sydney made me manager of Tito's which boasting a gaming licence, was able to offer roulette alongside top-class cabaret entertainment. We had Englebert Humperdink and Johnny Ray I recall. I sat with Johnny in the dressing room and we chatted a little, although I have to say he was a little down at the time, as he was doubling at Alison's Night Club in Bootle, also owned by Syd. I think Johnny felt he had hit an all time low with both venues as they were after all tiny places. I felt sorry for the man who had once graced concert rooms, a big star in his time. He actually shed a few tears as I spoke with him, but when he per-formed, he still was that world-class artist.

My next employer was Terry Phillips, a well known personality in Liverpool. He and his partner Frank Sharrocks owned Pick-wicks, Wooky Hollow and the Coconut Grove. I was made man-ager of these marvellous venues and had a wonderful time meeting the people, including Bill Davis who was to purchase Aintree Race-course. Bill gave me some great advice at the time, and I was always eager to learn from success. But more and more I wanted to become independent, I wanted to go it alone. I felt I had been second in command long enough, and it was now time I jumped on board my own ship of dreams, and steer them safely home.

At the time I was living in Liverpool's Buttermere Close, where my near neighbour was footballer Tommy Wright who became a personal friend. As did Colin Harvey, John Hurst, Roger Kenyon and Joe Royle. All these gentleman were to prove very supportive to my son Lawrence, who became an excellent football player. After a successful time playing for the local Schoolboy Associa-tions, playing in Germany on several occasions, Lawrence was asked to play for the town of Branau in Austria, to which he agreed, and in doing so, began to travel there just to play at weekends. It was a crazy idea, but it worked. Granada made a documentary about him too, and he became known as the young sportsman who travelled hundreds of miles a week just to play football. This was just so that he could be home for work Monday. His work by the way was to help his Dad set up his business. In the meantime he would taxi to Manchester airport, fly to Munich, be picked up by car, travel down to Branau and play on Saturday, then return on Sunday. Lawrence unfortunately suffered a broken leg in a school game which was to slow down his progress with Everton Football Club which he had joined as an apprentice.

On my side, I now had met up with a chap by the name of Glen Dean who, along with two gentlemen, owned several Bingo clubs in the Merseyside area. These were 'The Coliseum' in Bootle, 'The Grosvenor' in Stanley Road, 'The Victoria' in Cherry Avenue and 'The Royal' on Breck Road and the Mere Lane Cinema in Anfield. I managed all these venues and was now moving closer to the dream of owning my own establishment. From there I moved to the Essoldo Bingo Club in Southport, then to the Kingsway Club Southport which also owned the Grand Casino and Bingo club. Still I was restless, I wanted to be my own boss, but soon opportunity was going to come knocking.

Harry Dickinson was known as the Bingo King; he printed Bingo books and other entertainment products that were used in various premises in the Lancashire area. He also owned the Princess Bingo Club which he was running down with the intention of closing it. My big chance had arrived and Lady Luck had walked into my life, and the Lady was a Princess. I soon arranged a meeting with Harry and from there on we became good friends. I put it to Harry straight. I wanted to buy the Princess but I had no money. Not a great start you might think, but Harry took to me. I told him I would find the money somehow. I remember he nodded and gave me a little smile, then did something I am eternally grateful for. He introduced me to his own solicitor, a Mr Edwin Naylor who was to become a real family friend and guide me in so many ways on my road to independence. The loan was raised via our house in Buttermere Close, the Bank then issuing the grand sum of £1,500 to close the deal. At the time it seemed like an awful lot of money and I had some sleepless nights thinking about it. But there is always a price tag to any dream.

Life in the past hadn't always been easy for my family. I was after all very mobile as a Mecca Manager, then later as a trouble-shooter. Now, I could give my wonderful wife something more concrete, a future for us and our six children. We had two lovely daughters and four sons to be proud of. Now I would make up for the lost years.

By now we had moved house many times, and the children had moved schools. There had been disputes, but then all families have their problems, and beneath it all we were a strong family with love at its core.

The Princess Bingo Club became mine, and with all that has passed, I thank God, that Lil, my ex wife and son Lawrence are still in possession of the Princess. Looking back to the elation I felt in those early days, it's hard to believe what I allowed myself to become. In my drive for success, ambition must have changed me. I don't make any excuses. I know I am to blame. I left my wife, I broke my children's hearts. I only hope and pray that time will heal their pain and they will forgive me for everything I have done wrong.

So here began my entrepreneurial career. At the onset I called on all my Mecca experience and training, to set up systems that in the past had brought success. From there, with a handful of staff, which included a wonderful lady by the name of Mavis, who is still there to this day, we moved forward. It seems like Fast Forward looking back, and we did it in style too, with promotions that included Ken Dodd and many football personalities.

Life was looking good, and to my joy, my family had become involved in the business too. My wife Lil proving indispensable, as were my sons Lawrence and Gary and daughter Patsy. What more could I ask for? A happy Bank Manager! Well I had that too. He loved us. Our profits grew, as did our reputation as a successful family business.

The Armstrong family now had a house in Formby, a Bingo Club in Manchester, another in Wallasey, a canal side Marina club in Burscough and a Bingo club evolved from the empty Capitol cinema in Liscard. Later my son Lawrence was to obtain the lease of the Royal Bingo club and turn it into a snooker club. The premises had to be completely renovated to produce this change over but this also has been an excellent success for him.

But it was the Capital Bingo Club which was proving the most successful and on the back of its success, I used the upper part of the premises and opened a night club called 'The Capital Night Spot'. I was at the pinnacle of my career, a middle aged man with a good lifestyle, a wonderful wife and family, money in the bank. I felt good about life. But it was here at the Capital that my life was about to change forever.

I confess I am no angel. There have been other dalliances in my full life; the entertainment business put many temptations in my path and I didn't always step aside. But now Lady Luck was about to play me a wild card, a beautiful young woman was about to walk into my life and become my fatal attraction.

I know I only have myself to blame for my foolish heart. I chose a path, and I thought I was prepared for all the stumbling blocks that would come my way. How wrong I was! Nothing could have prepared me for the horror of being locked up for twenty three hours a day for a crime I didn't commit. Having my good name ruined by constant newspaper articles carrying my photographs, and slanderous accusations. But worst of all, losing all contact with my children. In writing this book I am trying to set the record straight, explaining to my children and family relations, of which there are many, what actually happened. When you and they have read my story, I hope at last the truth will be crystal clear to them and to you.

I accept I'm guilty of many things. I let my family down. I left a good wife who had seen me through all the bad years. But I have been punished for that in many ways. I lost everything. I will never recover, not here inside where it counts. All I can do now is prove I am innocent of the crime I was sentenced to serve seven years for. But let me go back to where it all started to go wrong.

Opposite the Capital Bingo Club was a public house called the Wellington Hotel owned by a John Grey. I had come to know John over the four weeks when alterations were being completed in the club, when me and some friends would often pop in for a drink.

About two months after our opening night, which incidentally was opened by Billy Butler from Radio Merseyside, who drew a crowd of around a thousand people - a full house!. I was in my office completing a new policy format for my other premises, when I heard a knock on my office door. I opened the door and there before me stood a young lady I recognised as John Grey's daughter. I called her in and she sat on a chair opposite my desk. We talked a little and she asked if I had a vacancy in the bar area. I told her I was not aware of a position, but would ask my son Lawrence who was manager there. She told me her name was Carol, and she seemed very confident for her young years and notably attractive.

Carol Tilbery started work the following Monday in our downstairs auditorium bar, and since she had some previous experience in the licensing trade she took to the work in a very competent manner. She was a good employee and I was a satisfied employer. This distance would soon be closed up and our lives entwined.

At the end of each evening I would be involved in receiving the takings and floats from the staff involved in the operation. Carol was one of those who would come to me. Over the next weeks we had many engaging conversations and on impulse one evening, I asked her to join me for an Indian meal at a nearby restaurant. I had taken other members of staff along with me for such meals; these were just social get-togethers, a time for relaxing. Carol was aware other staff members might tag along and so this was all very innocent.

Over the next few weeks I obtained a licence to open the upper level of the Capital as a night club, and so it was the Capital Night

Spot was born. I had now acquired a Mercedes 450 sports car and I suppose I felt very pleased with myself. I was also aware that Carol and I were becoming much closer, my attitude towards her now being one of suitor. She responded to my advances and I suppose our involvement was inevitable.

I now had my old pal John Morgan as manager at the Capital Night Spot, and I requested Carol be moved from the bar in the Bingo Club bar to the bar in The Capital Night Spot. I felt Carol with her personality and youth would prove a great asset to John and myself in promoting this new venue. Carol was very successful in this new role, and of course as we were now associating more frequently in work time, we grew closer. In retrospect, I now wonder what a girl of eighteen saw in a man of fifty two. Maybe it was my success or my money that attracted her, but then that short changes us both. I sincerely feel Carol did fall in love with me, as I did with her. It wasn't hard to fall in love with Carol. She became very attentive to my appearance, my meals, and my well-being. I was flattered and grew more interested in her. I mean no disrespect to my wife Lil, when I say these things, Lil had always been a de-voted wife. But over the years of travelling, I had become distant, a bit of a loner. Until this time, and for a few preceding years, I had been enjoying a love affair with ambition. Now my ambitious heart wanted Carol.

At first I felt a little sorry for her. She had told me she had married very young, a sweetheart from her school days. The marriage had not lasted; the couple had split after the death of their little baby. Carol was still deeply saddened by this and I felt great pity for her.

When does pity turn to passion? I don't know. I'm not wise enough to know that. I only know that passion can turn again to pity, for I pity her now. So we became lovers, and my heart was on a rollercoaster to disaster. At the time it seemed a perfectly sane thing I was doing, and why not? I was in control of the situation. I was an experienced man. How could anything go wrong?

****

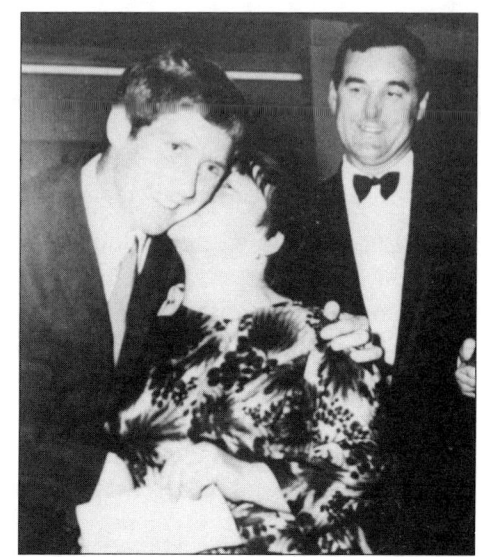

The 1960s

Top left: Bernard, alias Stan Ogden of Coronation Street fame.

Top right: With Alan Ball.

Bottom right: With Jimmy Clitheroe.

CHAPTER THREE
SELF MADE - SELF BETRAYED

ONCE those around us could see there was a relationship going on between us, there were words of warning proffered to me. Some were serious, others were more rye,

"Enjoy it while it lasts," some would say.

"It will end in tears," was another.

"Whose tears?" I wondered. I smiled, but couldn't tell them just how deep I was getting. On reflection I now see many people had my welfare at heart, but at the time all I could see was a young woman I wanted to possess. She made me feel young, virile, sexy. I had everything but I still wanted her.

The warnings I speak about also came from unlikely quarters. One night I was sitting in my office speaking to someone on the phone. As I chatted, the internal phone we had installed buzzed. I told my caller to hang on whilst I answered the internal phone. It was my security man saying that two men wanted to come up and talk to me. I said fine, but asked John Morgan my manager to accompany them to my office. I was rather surprised to see one of my visitors was John Grey with another younger man.

I smiled and invited them in. The younger man who looked sullen and just stared at me was introduced by John as James Tilbery, Carol's ex-husband. I was a little taken back by this, and I was puzzled as to why John had brought him there. We made small talk for a little while, then John said both he and James were aware of my involvement with Carol. This came as a surprise as up until then I thought we had been discreet with only a close number of people aware of the situation. My initial reaction was that they were there to tell me to leave her alone. I felt that any minute they were going to call me a dirty old man; deep down maybe that's how I felt. But then my pride inside said, 'You're not old - you're fifty two, not ninety two.' Guilt, our age difference, our illicit affair, the fact that I was cheating on my wife made me deaf, dumb and blind that day. I thought at the time they were warning me off, and were coming the heavy father and ex husband. I now realise they were not. What they were doing was warning me not to get involved with Carol. When they left they were fine and they displayed no animosity towards me at all. Still I didn't get it. No, I was far too self indulgent to see the writing on the wall.

The Royal Bingo club in King Street, Wallasey still belonged to me, and above it there was a luxury flat that had been renovated by the previous owner. I used to stay there when working late at the Capital. Now it became a love nest and I confess Carol and I continued our liaison, using the place quite frequently. The Royal was now of course defunct, and I had transferred the gaming licence to the Capital. This was something that had delighted me. You see, this had never been sanctioned before and was something of a first. With such good fortune and the attention of a beautiful young woman, I felt invincible. Who wouldn't?

It was around this time my old pal Don McCallion turned up on the scene. He now worked for EMI as an area Director, and it was great to see him again. Once old times were dusted away, I mentioned to him there had been quite a bit of interest in the Capital Bingo club from other Bingo operators. I asked him to give me an asking price so that I could quote to prospective purchasers. Don was very helpful, he came along to the Capital with a colleague and suggested the price should be set at £260,000. To paint a broader picture, I had a long lease on the property with an option to purchase. I was admitting approximately five to six thousand people a week and we were open seven afternoons and seven nights.

This was a very GOING concern. I was pleased with the estimated price and after careful consideration made up my mind to sell the Capital Bingo and the Capital Night Spot. Carol was behind me one hundred percent on this decision, as she had become a little restless at the Capital. We were working and playing together and perhaps it was a little claustrophobic for her. Because she was so young, I was always prepared to make allowances for that. Either way she seemed pleased things were changing.

Once the sale of the Capital had been arranged, I contacted a friend who had emigrated to America. I knew Carol wanted to see something of the States, and when alone we had talked of many things we would like to do together. Reckless as ever, I arranged for us both to go. It was a furtively arranged holiday, with us both arriving separately at the airport, and shamefully I used business as the excuse to my wife. In situations like this you kid yourself that no one will get hurt, but deception always has its victims.

Carol and I had a wonderful three weeks in America. Whilst there, we met Liverpool comedienne Faith Brown and her husband, and got along so well we made a foursome for the day visiting Disneyland. But the highlight for me was meeting and having coffee with the legendary George Raft, star of so many memorable films. We were staying at the Holiday Inn in Santa Monica at the time. The meeting came about through the kindness of a gentleman by the name of Eddie Simpson.

This world was light years from my days of delivering washing for my mother. Reality had slipped through my fingers and I was living a dream.

On returning to England, Carol and I decided to confirm our relationship by moving in together. We did so as soon as the Capital Bingo club was sold. The Royal was then passed over to my son Lawrence who converted it into a snooker hall. The Princess Bingo club was still mine and operating very successfully. But I decided to seek advice from my good friend and bank manager Mr Cotton, also my solicitor who had always been of great help to me and my family. Little did I know at that time that banks and solicitors were to feature more in my life from now on.

It was at this time that Carol told me she had become pregnant, which was shameful of me. But our love produced a wonderful boy we named Lee who I think the world of. I love all my children and regardless of all that has passed, I feel blessed that my love has produced such fine young men and women.

After the birth of Lee, we flew once again to America to discuss our future. Meantime I arranged to purchase a purpose built flat in New Brighton. On our return, I moved in with Carol until the flat was completed. I also bought a taxi business from an old friend Roy Digman - Wallasey Taxis. To boost business I purchased a fleet of Ford cars; at the time, the owner of Seaforth taxis was very helpful to me. So Carol and I had begun to create a new life together, but it was becoming an expensive lifestyle as I wanted to give Carol the best. She was young and impressionable and I doted on her and our new baby Lee.

To raise more money, I sold my collection of medals and other collectable war time items. I do regret doing that now, but at least I sold them to a personal friend who gave me a very fair price.

The money from my collection now purchased a five berth caravan - a Swedish model which had a tow bar that could be fitted to my Mercedes saloon. While the dust settled and my family and friends accepted my new life, Carol, Lee and I went touring in France and Spain for three months. It was whilst we were touring that the caravan door blew off and gave Carol a nasty crack on the head. We both thought it would be wise to get back home and have the bump looked at, so we returned to England via Southampton and then drove to Torquay. We stayed there two weeks, and Carol had her head examined. Thankfully it was alright which was a relief. From there we returned to Spain, visiting Barcelona and stayed away another two months. Reading this you'll think it sounds a little crazy, but then I suppose it was a little madness. I had reached an age where I should have known better, but there I was acting like a young man - Carol had made me young again.

When we returned to England, things had to be sorted out; I owed that to my wife Lil and my children but I knew that my future was going to be with Carol.

Carol and I now had moved into the New Brighton flat, and we had disposed of the caravan. I had talked things over with my wife and all that remained was to collect my clothing and personal items. From a legal standpoint I assigned our home at Meadow Court in Formby to Lil. I also transferred all my business assets to my sons Lawrence and Gary. This was a little sanity in my world, and I thank God I did that.

I was virtually starting again, making a new life. I approached my bank manager Mr Cotton who arranged a loan for me. This would cover the flat in New Brighton, the taxi business and a new project I had stumbled on.

The Grand Hotel in New Brighton was a 30-bedroom hotel which I purchased from a friend named Peter Catchpole. This proved a marvellous success and did very well for us. There were several bars, a good residential trade plus a growing entertainment side and discotheque. Two old friends gave me a lot of help and advice at that time; they were Bob Wooler of Cavern DJ fame, and Allan Williams, the Beatles first manager. There was always something happening at the Grand - never a dull moment. One night I was on duty at our discotheque door, when I saw a man trying various car doors in the car park. I walked up to the man and asked what he was doing. To my horror he pulled out a gun from his waistband. I froze - aware that this might be it. He then oddly pulled out a cheque and asked me to cash it. Naturally I said I would, but told him I would have to go inside and get the money. He nodded and I quickly strode inside and rang the police. He had gone when they arrived, but they did arrest him a little later that night after he had tried the same line with someone at a club not too far from us.

My taxi business had gone from strength to strength and it was at this time that New Brighton Taxi's approached me with an offer to buy out the business. As my interests in the Grand kept me busy enough, I agreed, and disposed of this area of business. On completion of the sale I purchased The Gaiety Night Club in West Houghton, near Bolton. We also disposed of our lovely flat and took a smart detached house in Westhoughton. This was a pretty exclusive estate just outside the town. We had the house refurbished throughout and Carol loved it there. Lee was now attending nursery school which allowed Carol to assist me during the day. So once again all seemed to be moving along very smoothly.

The Gaiety was developed into a Bingo club and night club. How we did this was programming Bingo from 1 p.m. until 9.30 p.m. Then I would bring in cleaners, re arrange the layout and it became a cabaret club until 2.0 a.m. This all worked out perfectly with no problems at all.

It was during this time that Carol and I developed a love for a place called Los Gigantis in the Canary Isles. We had taken to shooting off there for little breaks. I've always worked hard; now I was playing hard, maybe making up for lost time. Carol was young and seemed to become restless and sought change, and I didn't mind at all our flights of fancy.

Over the following months I came to purchase the Tiffany ballroom in Wigan, and sold my interests in the Gaiety. Tiffany's was a Mecca trade name so I changed the name to Maxims, and again business boomed. The place held about 1,300 people. After a complete revamp and refurbishment we went to town engaging top star names. One top rate group we had was the Drifters, a superb act and a sellout night. But for me that booking brings back nothing but hellish memories.

Carol and I had started to have disputes about the irregular hours I had to work to keep us in the high lifestyle we had grown accustomed to. We were after all running three cars, a Mercedes sports, a Porsche, and a BMW. We also liked to fly frequently abroad for holidays, buy nice things and retain a wardrobe of fashionable clothes. The dream had to be paid for. Sadly these disputes flowed over into our work, and one particular argument took place the night the Drifters were booked at the club. I was upset about this and drank a little too much champagne in a bid to forget.

After the show, everyone, including my staff and friends moved to a friend's hotel where we celebrated a fine evening's work. We had after all had a full house and taken quite a lot of money. All seemed well and I stuck to champagne, the others guests drinking whatever they liked. What I didn't realise was that my champagne was being spiked with vodka. I became quite ill at one point and a close friend suggested he should arrange for Carol and me to be taken home.

When we got back, Carol raised Cain with me, but I was feeling too ill to answer back. The next thing I remember is going to the bathroom to be sick, Carol still shouting abuse and me half heartedly arguing back. From there I remember nothing until I awoke in Bolton Hospital. I was kept there a week with a broken leg and a badly damaged spine, which still affect me and always will. To this day, the accident remains a mystery. Yes, I know I was drunk, but how I came to fall down those stairs still haunts me.

In hospital my family came to visit me, including my son Gary. As always they showed their love for me and were concerned for my well being.

Whilst I was in hospital, Carol had taken over the running of Maxims which seemed to make sense. I felt she was capable until my return. Things however were not fine at all.

My staff informed me that a large sum of money had gone missing from the Drifters' income. The sum would later prove to be between five and six thousand pounds. I couldn't believe it, but I could only blame myself for this fiasco which was the result of my lackadaisical attitude. The loss of that money, like my fall, went into my book of unsolved mysteries.

It took many weeks for me to recover from my accident. I was using crutches and a walking frame to gain strength to walk again.

I slowly recovered but have become somewhat disabled from the injuries which still cause me great discomfort at times.

When I did eventually get back to work, Carol started to take Lee off for several days at a time to Merseyside. I have no idea where she stayed but she did this on several occasions. At the time, I thought it was a display of independence. I felt she thought she was getting back at me for the odd hours I had to keep in order to run a successful business. It was then that I heard the Pavilion Bingo club was available for purchase. I had operated the Pavilion when I was employed by Mecca and so I knew this was a great place with lots of potential. I wasted no time in arranging a meeting with Mecca officials in London. On my return, I talked things over with Carol and she seemed very keen on the idea of moving again and our relationship seemed a little better now.

The next move was disposal of the lease of Maxims, which came about through a good friend, Carl Eaden who had been a working colleague at such places as Pickwicks and the Coconut Grove. So when he took over the lease of Maxims, it was a pleasure dealing with him. Within our negotiations, I talked about my problems at home and somehow the night of my accident came up. It was then that Carl confirmed that he had seen who had spiked my champagne with vodka. He said it was Carol. I was shocked, but it was a thought that had crossed my mind over the previous months. But there was worse to come. Whilst having one of our heated arguments I accused Carol of pushing me down those stairs and nearly killing me. I hoped she would tell me the idea was rubbish, but her reply was. "I'd do it again". Our relationship was now on a slippery slope and I was only thankful we had not married.

It was now that I took possession of the Pavilion Bingo Club in Lodge Lane. As Carol seemed to be making more effort, we decided to try again and we moved into a bungalow which I had purchased in Magull. Lee was now enrolled into Mount Carmel School near Ormskirk, which he thoroughly enjoyed. Lee had his sixth birthday whilst we lived in the bungalow - I still have the video. So yes, there were happy times too. But the happy times were always interspersed with rows which sometimes blew up out of all proportion. On one occasion I had taken Carol to see a show; we returned home where Doris Grey, Carol's mother, was baby sitting. We had not been in long when a disagreement developed between us. I was sitting down at the time facing Doris Grey, when Carol suddenly hit me on the head with the telephone. I fell forward with a terrible gash to my head, the wound bleeding very badly. Doris called 999 for an ambulance. While we waited for the ambulance, Doris rushed for a towel and held it to my head. Carol remained unmoved by it all. Next, I was taken to Walton Hospital where the wound was attended to. This blow kept me away from business for several days. As I avidly keep all paperwork, a habit formed through business, I still have details of that hospital visit.

So back to work again. I was now the freehold owner of the Pavilion and I had as my manager John Morgan who had long ago first introduced me to the world of entertainment. There was no time to lick wounds, as we had to get this baby off the ground. But this wasn't the only baby that was going to need my attention. Carol now told me she was pregnant. I was floored, and my feelings leapt from panic to elation. I was already the father of six children by marriage to my wife Lil. Then there had been the two children prior to my marriage. Now here in later life I was to become a father yet again.

I now had to think things over very carefully. Lee and this new baby were to be labelled illegitimate, and yet their parents were together in spite of our stormy affair. Being older, my view is still rather conservative; I was uncomfortable with it. I suppose I felt guilty that I had not given them my name. I talked with Carol, and I also talked with my solicitor Edward Naylor. I had talked with Mr Naylor on other occasions about my volatile relationship with Carol and he had rightly pointed out to me, that Carol's behaviour probably stemmed from insecurity. He felt that she may have these aggressive feelings because she was still legally not my wife. His remedy was divorce Lil and marry Carol. It seemed to make sense and Carol appeared calmer and grew more beautiful each day as we awaited our new baby.

Meanwhile Mr Naylor talked with Lil and divorce was now spoken of with great seriousness. I had left Lil and my family, in 1979, after becoming deeply involved with Carol after the birth of Lee.

It seemed incredible that seven years had elapsed and it was now 1986. Lil was wonderful about everything and helped all she could to conclude this sad passing of our long marriage.

Carol and I had a quiet wedding at Crosby Town Hall. My old pal Carl Eaden was best man. Later the wedding party went on to a celebration dinner, my good friend Ron Davies taking memorable photographs which I still have in my possession.

Before the birth of our new baby we sought the advice of a Dr Francis, an eminent gynaecologist. We found we needed very careful advice because it had come to light on the birth of Lee that Carol had been born with several kidney problems. We were going to need great care and guidance. Unknown to me, Carol had been advised not to conceive again after Lee. I truly was unaware of this and was very worried when he told me that bearing children with the problems she had was detrimental to her health. I was shocked in fact. Thankfully Carol gave birth to a healthy baby boy at Dr Francis' private clinic, but the warning was now firmly given to me. Dr Francis took me to one side and said, "George, Carol must never become pregnant again. I am afraid if she does it could seriously affect her health and well-being".

I was horror struck. I knew I must never put her through that again. We both love children, but now I knew I must take precautions and be sure Carol would not become pregnant again. It was hard to face up to this sad predicament. It wasn't so bad for me, I was older. I knew the joy of children by my first wife Lil but Carol was still young. It was such a tragedy that bearing children could be so damaging for her. This was worrying news, but nothing could spoil the joy of our new baby Jonathan, a real big bundle of joy.

So once again we tried for a new beginning. We were now man and wife with a fine home and growing business. In fact the Pavilion was doing so well, we installed a chip shop which served patrons in the Bingo hall and passing trade outside. Above the Pavilion were the old Mecca offices, from where I created the Pivvy Bar night club. Again this proved a wonderful success and good investment. The Pivvy was managed by my old friend Doris, whose husband is a ship's chief engineer. They are two lovely people who generated a lot of business for me, and I was proud of them and my bar.

Business was so good in the Bingo hall. In fact five thousand patrons or so were coming into us each week, and with good staff on board, Carol and I took a late honeymoon in our favourite Los Gigantis. We still had our ups and downs but I was prepared to sweep things under the carpet. We had our new little boy Jonathan keeping us occupied, and being around such a package of goodness, it was easy to forgive a lot. Lee loved his new brother and there were times I hoped things would work out. In an effort to give the marriage more time, I began neglecting my business interests. On reflection, I had been acting pretty stupidly for some time, and I could see I had been blown whichever way the wind blew to try and keep Carol happy. I had sold the Capital Bingo club for far less than it was worth, I had let the discotheque above go for buttons, the same could be said for the taxi business. I just had not been using my head, and now in trying once more to keep the relationship going, to establish home life and stability for the four of us, I had jeopardised all that I had striven for.

Carol once again wanted to move house, feeling that Southport would prove a better environment. At the time my three sons Gary, Carl and Lawrence were living there. As always, I did everything Carol wanted. I still loved her, and I worshipped our two boys. What else could a man do? I wanted her to be happy. We searched and soon came up with a lovely property known as *Villa Allegra*, and what a home it was! A superb bungalow set in several acres with its own indoor swimming pool. But you can't always get what you want, and this sale hit snags as property deals often do, and the sale fell through. But Carol was to have her Southport address, when quite by chance we heard of a property becoming available on Fleetwood Road. The house overlooked the golf course and once Carol was inside she said, "This is it." And on that happy note we proceeded to purchase the house and arrange a total refurbish. Carol was excellent in choosing all the right colours for our home; she had great insight for colour schemes and created a beautiful home for us. The house by the way had a wonderful garden. The previous owner had been a builder and had spent money and the best materials to create a delightful garden. Unfortunately it had become overgrown and in need of care. I made sure it was given that loving care it needed and me and my pal Mr Tege completely renovated it. The very large pond was brought to life when at the end I purchased a dozen or so very large Japanese coy fish. It was a marvellous sight and a real labour of love.

Another good thing happened while we were living there - my sons Gary and Lawrence visited us. I was so pleased about this as it can't have been easy for the boys. In their eyes I had walked away from their world but they were old enough and wise enough not turn their back on me. I thank God for that.

But all the new houses, beautiful gardens, fine clothes and good holidays can't hold a marriage together unless love is in their too. Sadly love seemed to slipping away.

Carol and I once again seemed to be arguing more and more, and our relationship deteriorated and became at times a nightmare . It's hard to pin-point a time when it started to get worse, but Carol had taken up a friendship with a lady by the name of Janis who lived near Crossens, on the outskirts of Southport. I was told she was a part-time model. Either way Carol started to disappear once again and we had more upsets. By now I had become accustomed to these breakaway days and nights but it was tiring me. I was too old for this. There was after all thirty years difference between us and it was beginning to tell on me. But I'm not one to give up easily and I felt that maybe if we had a holiday in Los Gigantis it might bring some love back into our failing marriage. Carol agreed and we went away for three weeks. I have to say on the whole it was a success. We came home refreshed and ready to try again, or so I thought. In no time Carol was out at night with her new friend Janis. In fact Carol frequented her house daily. Like a fool I found myself putting up with this, and I was now playing mother and father to Lee and Jonathan and in so doing neglected business. I really didn't know which way to turn. How could this be happening to me? I could control business; I had proved to be a successful entrepreneur, but there I was at home letting my young wife treat me like a puppet and making our marriage a sham. I was ashamed that I had no control over what my wife was doing. I thought if I gave her all that freedom she would come round and eventually settle down.

For my part, I endeavoured to keep my business interests on a solid footing, but I had been neglectful of late. If it had not been for John Morgan, my manager. I would have been in dire straits financially. John kept the ship afloat for me.

In a desperate attempt to keep our marriage going, we took another holiday in Los Gigantis. Just one more last chance at pulling our life together. But the holiday turned out to be a disaster in more ways than one. Events ahead were going to change our lives. The year was 1986; the month was March. We had been on holiday two weeks when I received a call from home. It was dreadful news. The Pavilion Bingo Club, along with my night club, had been destroyed in a major fire. Even the little chip shop had been lost. It was so bad that flats and shops nearby had been evacuated in fear of further damage. I was devastated. I arranged immediately for a flight home. That time was so depressing for us. As if things weren't bad enough between us, now came financial loss and all the stress that entailed.

Once home, I left Carol and the boys and went to view the damage. It was a chilling sight, I felt very sad at the passing of this beautiful theatre. This fine hall of entertainment, a grand old lady that had seen all the greats pass by her. Stars such as Gracie Fields,

Paul Robeson, Ken Dodd, The Beatles. They had all been on her stage. The old building had survived the war, even the Toxteth riots which had taken out many buildings in its wake. The Pavilion had never been touched. Not even a broken window. But now the curtain had come down on her, and she lay in ruins. Little did I realise I would soon be the next to fall.

After extensive investigation by the police and the fire services, it was discovered that the fire had been caused by an electrical fault, the seat of the fire being placed on the stage of the Bingo club. Thankfully no one had been in there. By the time the fire had taken hold it was apparently nearing midnight. However, the night club above the Bingo club had been full. So casualties could have arisen if the authorities had not acted quickly to evacuate everyone successfully. I am so grateful for that blessing. I had nighmares thinking about how terrible things might have been. For all the heartache the fire was to bring, I thanked God that no one had been hurt.

****

CHAPTER FOUR
THE LAW AND THE DISORDER

WHEN the company that handled the insurance was contacted with information, I was about to meet with another major disaster. They had made a grave mistake with regard to the insurance of the Pavilion. Little did I know how bad things were going to get. The value of my property and income had professionally been assessed by a very well known institution from London, and it had been clearly stated that it would cost somewhere in the region of two million pounds to rebuild the Pavilion. But that was only a building; it could never be the same. The shock of losing the Pavilion was tremendous, but there was far worse to come. Carol and I were just not working out at all, and our marriage now mirrored the ruinous embers of the Pavilion. Disconsolate, I placed my claim in the hands of my legal representatives and old friend Edward Naylor who was aware of my business and personal problems.

I was told that the insurance company advised me to obtain other premises as soon as I could. I acted on this advice and looked at several properties, but they were all out of town and I wanted to stay close by my family. I knew Lee and Jonathan needed me to be close by. Carol on the other hand was now making it clear that she did not need me. By now she was disappearing more frequently and when she was at home her behaviour towards me was hostile. Her violent outbursts often resulted in injury to me. You may find this hard to believe, but it is the truth and I have hospital documentation to prove what I say is true.

So now my property and business had been consumed in a terrible fire, just as my heart had been consumed in a terrible passion for Carol. Both now were smouldering cinders, the black smoke of despair choking everything around me. How could there be anything else that could bring me lower than this time I asked myself? Well I soon found out when Carol informed me that she was pregnant. I was flabbergasted. How could this be? I had been taking precautions to ensure there would be no more children. It was just too painful to face the obvious, but I kept my thoughts to myself. But now Carol's mood and attitude grew colder towards me and her temper had now reached out at our children.

One evening Jonathan and Lee were in the bath and they were fooling about as youngsters often do. Jonathan slipped however and it resulted in Carol striking Lee across his face with a wet towel. Lee had the most awful swelling on his nose and forehead from this attack and next day we had to keep him off school. Carol took Jonathan off to his nursery school and went over to her friend Janis's where it seemed she spent many, many days.

Meantime, life went on. My bank was very patient waiting for settlement of my insurance claim but my own personal money was starting to run out, and there were debts running up due to business commitments taken whilst at the Pavilion. Things seemed to be getting worse. I now had to take Lee out of his private school as I could no longer meet the fees. Next, the cars had to go.

It was now clear that Carol could not put up with our new situation. She had been used to the good life, and now things had gone sour for us, she turned her anger towards me. Her outbursts now led to her smashing things about the house and frankly I had taken enough. I had tried all the way with her; I had explained that things would get better once the insurance people had settled with me. Still she remained hostile, and on several occasions taunted me with regard to her forthcoming baby. More than once she had said to me, and I quote "What makes you think it is yours?" What indeed, but I just couldn't face that possibility. Then she began staying away from home more and more, and fool that I was, I still thought that perhaps it was due to her pregnancy, and the worry of our financial status. Being pregnant and not having the good things in life was a culture shock for her, for me too for that matter but I could cope.

I felt at a loss as to what to do next, but I knew there was only one recourse. I would seek a divorce. I had pushed it so often to the back of my mind but now I felt that it really was the only option. Besides, I was now becoming convinced the baby she carried could not be mine. I was tortured by this, but in my heart I so wanted it to be our baby. I was still kidding myself.

In April 1988, I visited my solicitor Mr Naylor who put me in touch with a Mr Calder, a divorce solicitor within Allan Jones and Allan, Mr Naylor now being amalgamated with this firm since the death of his partner. Mr Calder proceeded with the relevant documentation and informed Carol that I had requested a divorce. Carol was quite taken aback by this move, and her response was another outburst. In fact she went off once again for two days whilst I was left to attend to the children. Maybe she needed time to clear her mind but either way she seemed to have quietened down a little when she returned. The dust settled and I went about trying to find suitable business premises and make a start at rebuilding my business life. The property I eventually came by was the Victoria Bingo Club in Cherry Avenue, Liverpool 11.

On Carol's side of things, she had now obtained the services of a divorce solicitor. I was later to be informed his name was Roy Brown with Smethers Warpole and Smethers based in Liverpool. So it was acknowledged that divorce proceedings had commenced. We still lived however in the same house and agreed to do so until we parted. At this juncture Mr Brown, my wife's solicitor, froze all my assets. Obviously included in that sum, was the two million pounds payable to me, from the insurance company. I was sixty two years old, and suddenly I felt those years heavy on my shoulders. But I could not throw in the towel yet. While you're still on your feet you can always bounce back off the ropes, that is, if it's a fair fight. But I was to find the punches were going to come fast and furious, all of them below the belt.

Back to business, I told my solicitor that I had managed to obtain the chance of another Bingo Club. He told me I would need the sanction of my wife's solicitor Mr Brown.

Mr Brown responded with a letter that said yes, as long as Carol was given a fifty per cent share, but she would have no responsibility in running the business.

My solicitor was shocked at this request, so was I. Our response back was brief. FORGET IT, we told them. As a matter of interest, you may like to know that at my first trial, Justice Crowe was shown this letter from Mr Brown, and commented that it was clearly a blackmail letter.

But now, at home, something new started to occur. Mr Brown started to ring my wife. The calls were frequent, but more puzzling was the fact they were in the evening, between 8.30 and 10.30. However, the divorce was proceeding and so I was not unduly worried. I had my business interests to look to.

My son Lawrence and my first wife Lillian had obtained a Bingo club called the Carlton, on Moss Lane, Orrell Park. They agreed to let me have it via the insurance claim, which was due to be settled by the High Court in Manchester.

I took possession of the Carlton and started to regenerate it into a successful business. Slowly Carol, the two children and I started to regain our status. Still yet again we were to be thwarted.

We were called to the High Court in Manchester with regard to my insurance claim on the Pavilion Theatre. To be brief, the Company who were charged to look after the insurance of the business had failed to renew the cover for the building. The renewal date was January the 4th 1986, the fire took place in March 1986. The Company was Inept and Crucked and Co of Aintree. The court advised that if I enforced bankruptcy on this company, I would gain nothing. They suggested I take a settlement offer of £100,000 plus costs. I was crushed by this news, and in desperation I accepted this settlement, only to find out later that I could have taken the Company and its Directors to the dry cleaners. In a word, I had acted like an idiot, but then I had placed my trust in advisors I thought knew better. My world was becoming like some bad dream, except that you wake up from a bad dream. Soon my life was going to take a long journey into night, and the nightmare would never end.

So now I had to dispose of the Carlton Bingo Club to enable my legal representatives to pay off my creditors and I was back at Square One.

At home, life was still difficult. Carol and I argued constantly. Her temper tantrums, and her violent outbursts were no way abated by the fact she was heavily pregnant. I confess that at her request she had the police keep me in the station on more than one occasion. Carol wanted me out of the house, and it had got that sometimes she just couldn't bear the sight of me. I should have moved out then, but there were the boys and the baby she was having. I felt I just couldn't leave her like that. I did not realise at the time she already had set her cap at Roy Brown. Soon however I would be made aware of a growing liaison.

One night when Carol and I were watching television - there were calm waters between the storms- the telephone rang. I picked it up to hear the now-familiar voice of Mr Brown wanting to speak to Carol. I handed the phone to her and she went into the kitchen to talk in private. During her talk she came into the lounge to collect some papers, and then returned to finish her call. I sat and sipped the wine we had been enjoying together. When she returned, I asked her what was all that about. She said that Mr Brown had enquired about the children's dates of birth. I accepted that and thought no more about it. Later she said she was going to bed; she did so, but not long after I could hear her talking on our portable vodaphone. I assumed she was talking to a friend and thought no more of it. I then cleared the bottle and our glasses to the kitchen, and as I entered I noticed a letter beside the telephone. I could see it was on headed note paper and from the office of Roy Brown. Human nature being as it is, I read it. I couldn't believe what I read. At the time I thought Carol had left it as an oversight. Now I am quite sure she left it there quite deliberately. I still have this letter, the contents of which are very damning to both him and Carol. In this letter he spoke of her unborn baby as David, and his attitude is far more attentive than the client-solicitor association. The letter is dated June 3rd 1988. Later Carol would taunt me by asking if I had noticed the kiss Mr Brown had secretly placed within his signature. For even now I was still oblivious to the extent of the deception. I was however realising there must be something going on. My first thought was to go and see him. I wanted to see what this man looked like. I knew Carol could have her pick of men as she is a very attractive lady, and I was always proud to be her husband. I felt honoured that she had chosen me.

I went along to see Mr Brown at his office. I was really curious to meet the man who was calling my wife so frequently. We were after all still legally married. Yes, I accepted the divorce - I had instigated it. But who was this man who seemed to be more than a solicitor to my wife? I had to find out.

I spoke to the receptionist and requested to see Mr Brown. The young lady asked for my name. In my hand I held the letter that spoke of David, and at the top of the letterhead was a name of a solicitor who also worked there. I told the girl my name was Benson.

She buzzed through with the message and soon Mr Brown came into the reception area. I took a good look at him. I was surprised. He was six foot six inches tall, white-faced and very thin. His ill fitting suit hung on him, and it was obviously of poor quality. Surely this cannot be someone Carol would be interested in I thought. Still not aware who I was, he invited me into his office, a poky back room which to me indicated he wasn't doing all that well. I sat opposite him and thought, 'If this is the best she can do, God help my children.' This may appear conceited, maybe it is, but at least I'm telling you the honest truth - that's how I read it.

We sat opposite each other across a desk. He seemed relaxed until I asked him why he was ringing up my wife so often at night. He shot up and said, "I know who you are - you're George Armstrong and if you don't leave, I will call the police." I stood up and was surprised to see that Mr Brown appeared quite shocked that I had visited him there. I think I gave him rather a bad fright, although why this six foot six man should be frightened of me I don't know. I was in my sixties; I stand about five six and since my fall was not as fit as I would like to have been.

On leaving his office I went over to my own solicitor and asked them to send a letter of apology regarding my intrusion. I shouldn't have gone there I know, but I was concerned with what was going to happen with regard to the children. If there was a new man in her life he was going to come in contact with my boys. After meeting Roy Brown I was sure he wasn't her type. How wrong can you be?

When Carol knew I had visited Brown, she blew her top. I naturally called him a drip, but Carol seemed to jump to his defence. This in itself should have told me volumes.

Later Mr Brown was to declare in various newspapers that "The Magic Moment in life was when he met Carol Armstrong".

Life is strange. In all this mess there came a little miracle. Carol gave birth to our third son. His name? Yes, David. A beautiful baby, but unlike our other two boys who are both dark haired with brown eyes, he had beautiful white blonde hair and clear blue eyes. Both Carol and I have brown eyes and so I found it hard to believe the child was mine. But none of that mattered. I held him, I kissed him; it was love at first sight. But passions were burning brightly. Little did I realise our time together was limited. Soon he would be pulled away from me. The last time I saw him he was crying whilst I stood there holding his dummy. But there was no time for goodbyes.

To this day I still carry his dummy in my pocket. But there was much more to come before that particular heartbreak. I was no longer deaf and blinded by love, but I was still a little dumb.

After the incident with the phone call, the letter I had found and my subsequent visit to see Brown, it became clear that Mr Brown and my wife were involved in a relationship. Whilst our divorce was being heard at court he escorted her there. Whilst this in itself is innocent enough, the continued calls between them intimated a closer bond than that of client-solicitor.

On the home front Carol had said her friend Janis could get her some modelling work. She said it would help a lot with our finances. I couldn't argue with that as things were tight. She seemed very perked by this new idea, and said the boys could get modelling work too. They would be perfect for catalogues. Firstly though she said she wanted to improve her looks. In particular her teeth. It really doesn't matter where this idea came from. As always I went along with every whim and fancy and I arranged for an appointment with my dentist Mr Chu; he went about recapping her teeth to their model form of today. Next I contacted an old pal, a professional photographer to take promotional shots of Carol and the boys.

They were wonderful shots, and I was proud of what I saw. But I was only looking at images. For all the world it looked as though Carol was a happy mum with her three sons. Behind the smile there were storms brewing. Maybe Carol wanted to be an independent woman of the world. Perhaps she hated the fact that I was the one who had provided her with so much. This modelling idea would at least give her a career of her own.

Carol was taken on by a top model agency in Manchester. All credit to her she seemed to be doing well. Even little Lee was given a handful of assignments with her. But it was her solo work that began to take her away more and more.

Maybe I had kidded myself that if I let her go her own way, one day she would come back to me. Crazy, I know, but somewhere in me the flame still flickered. I knew we were in a divorce, I knew she had not been faithful. But she was the mother of my boys, and a corner of my heart still held on to the better times we had shared. That corner however would slowly be chiselled away as Carol and her attentive solicitor stood against me.

In time the three of us would gather in court. The first experience was astonishing, and I couldn't believe how awful it was turning out. I was honestly embarrassed with the statements that had been concocted against me. For example, I had broken Carol's nose three times, split her head twice and given her numerous black eyes. All these things apparently transpired early on in our relationship! It was ridiculous. If that had been true, why oh why would she have agreed to marry me in 1986. We had been together since 1979 and in better times enjoyed wonderful holidays, had four lovely homes, luxury cars, in fact everything that money could buy and more. She had a husband that adored her, and three healthy boys. Why she had made up all these lies about me I'll never know. But then there was a new man in her life, a man who seemed only too eager to assist her.

At one very important court meeting I simply refused to appear. I had applied for custody of our children. Mr Brown replied - I still have that reply. I was told that if I withdrew my application, they would allow me finance via my bank to purchase a business. I discussed this offer with my solicitor who suggested I withdrew my application and take the chance to start a business. As soon as I had done so they obtained custody of the children.

By now I had been legally ejected from my home and was living in the *Prince of Wales*, a very expensive experience. I still called home to take Lee to school and Jonathan to his day nursery. From there I travelled to Kirkby where I had managed to acquire The Cherryfields Bingo and Social Club.

My hands were tied. I had to deal with things on a daily basis. However, I bit the bullet and put my mind back to business, and all seemed to be moving smoothly. It was inevitable I couldn't maintain the price of staying at the *Prince*. For a short time my ex-wife Lil let me stay with her. She now had a good relationship going with a man of her own age, and so it was very good of them to let me stay there. Not many women would have done that, but then Lil is golden.

But now, after a few weeks there came another odd request. Carol suggested I should move back into Fleetwood Road. This surprised me, for I had been told by Lee that Carol had been entertaining a man there by the name of Mike Whitewash. In fact he and some other friends had taken Carol and the boys out for a slap up meal. The man however turned out to be Carol's cousin, a Mr Mike Whitewash. He was a few years older than Carol and so I thought at first he was acting as some family advisor. However this was not the case. It transpired that Carol and he were involved in a close relationship. This is not supposition on my part. I know this to be true for I have in my possession a copy of a statement he made to the police confirming that involvement. But let me tell you how I came to come in contact with Mr Whitewash.

In May 1989, Doris Grey, Carol's mother, suggested that Mr Whitewash might be able to arrange for me to meet Carol to discuss the upkeep of the children and the disposal of the house. I agreed to meet him at his home in a suburb of Southport. I arrived at his home at 9.30 a.m. When he opened the door, he looked the worse for wear, his appearance rough and dishevelled. He was also drunk. He said a guest had stayed overnight and that was why he was in that state. After he invited me in, he looked at me with blurred vision and spoke with slurred speech. Our discussion commenced and in passing I asked him why he thought Carol had said in her divorce statement that her mother was dead. In the statement I speak of, Carol had said her mother had died of cancer, God only knows why!. Mr Whitewash blew his top at this remark in spite of his condition, his mother was the sister of John Grey, Carol's father, and so he could hardly believe this was true.

When he was ready, we proceeded to my home in Fleetwood Road from which I had been ejected. Mr Whitewash drove his

Volvo car regardless of my suggestion he was not really up to it. We did incidentally stop at a hotel on the way to have a coffee - he in fact had a large scotch and I had the coffee. I now think this stop off was an opportunity to ring and tell Carol that I was coming over with him. At this point, remember, I had no idea they were close company, and anyway it was none of my business - my concern was for the children.

On our arrival at Fleetwood Road there was no response to our ring of the bell or our knock at the door; there was no-one in. So the visit was a waste of time. Whitewash suggested I call at his home in the evening when he would arrange for Carol and me to meet and talk things over. I agreed. From there I went to my business in Kirkby, and Whitewash went to a pub in Churchtown. That is what he stated in his police statement.

At 6.30 that night I went along to Mr Whitewash's home, thinking we would be then going on to Fleetwood Road for a meeting with Carol. But to my surprise, there in the drive was Carol's car. I knocked the door several times before it was opened by Carol. No sooner had she done so than Mr Whitewash appeared and became abusive. He then lunged towards me. It was obvious that he was very drunk - in fact he fell as he came forward and pulled me to the ground. I was shocked. He of course was a man in his 30's whilst I was 62. As soon as I could, I got to my feet and left. I never returned or ever spoke to the man again. But the story didn't end there. He reported me to the police. For what ? I hadn't done anything. So next thing that happens is that I find myself making a statement to the police as to why I had visited Mr Whitewash. I gave them the facts as to why I had gone there, pointing out at the same time that Mr Whitewash had been extremely drunk. In fact you may be interested to know that when the police answered Mr Whitewash's call, they hadn't taken a statement from him; they went back a week later for it.

More intriguing, it was Mike Whitewash who had introduced Carol to Roy Brown, when he had used Mr Brown for his own divorce petition.

When the dust had settled, and there was plenty of it, I returned to Fleetwood Road. My son Lee and Jonathan had asked for me to go back home. I agreed to this and Carol and I thought it would be good for the children until the house was sold. It was also to prove useful to her when she took to disappearing for she knew I would always be there for them. It was not easy to explain to two small boys why mummy slept in one room and daddy in another, but then this is only one of the small problems in situations like this.

In this time I tried to re-establish myself in a business stance, whilst my wife continued her modelling assignments. Lee, being the oldest was aware of the problems of our marriage, and even little Jonathan, I'm sure, was beginning to understand all was not well.

The bonus of this awful time was that I was to spend more and more time with the children who were my joy and consolation. For all that was wrong in my life, these three boys lifted my heart.

Carol however was becoming more difficult, her feelings towards me and the children were uninspired. I could take that but it was unfair to the children. This situation would later escalate and worsen. As time went on my wife made more and more excuses that she had to go out; modelling could take her away for a couple of days. Then there were the friends she would visit. We were divorcing and so I accepted she was making her own life, but often she was not considering our boys. I was trapped - I had to be there for my sons. Financially I was in no position to make great changes and I had been foolish to let her gain eventual custody.

But there was a frightening new turn now; she threatened to kill herself and the boys. This suicide threat can be confirmed by a doctor and two welfare officers who visited us at this time. It was during this period that Carol had started physically assaulting me and the children. I was accustomed to this but I could not have her hurting the boys.

This lack of care also put David and Jonathan at some risk. Whilst she was enjoying her affair with Mr Brown, she left the two boys in a student apartment house with an unqualified minder. This was not just for a few hours either. They would be left from Friday till Monday. At this time I was under the impression she had them with her. When I was informed by a student that the boys would cry continuously, I took down the address and went and collected them and brought them home. At this time David was eighteen months old, Jonathan only three.

Now dear reader, let me tell you that at both my trials in Crown Court, none of this evidence was put forward in my defence. Maybe it was thought not relevant to the case. What do you think ?

There were 14 witnesses who wanted to speak on my behalf - they too were thought irrelevant. I could prove Carol had assaulted me and our son Lee continuously, also that her first husband, James Tilbery had left her because of her violent outbursts that would result in a physical attack. Then there were the people that would swear on oath that there were also other men that associated with my wife, even whilst she was carrying on an affair with Mr Brown. Still this information was brushed under that very big carpet. I wonder why? Perhaps it had something to do with the Rotarian association Mr Brown was associated with, or perhaps it was the closed ranks of the law. You can be the judge as we move along the very tangled threads of the law and secret societies.

At the time it was not only the prosecution that sank me; it was my defence. My solicitor's clerk, Mr Red was aware of all of this information, and he also knew my wife held three different driving licences, one in the name of Tilbery, another Grey, the other in her married name of Armstrong. All were being used, but the joke is my wife never held a full licence. I was not aware of this until she had left our home to join her boyfriend. If I had, I would never have trusted her with our boys. But there were many more things that were kept secret, perhaps more than I will ever know.

During our divorce proceedings, it came out that Mr Brown had known my wife longer than I had realised, but we shall come to that later. For now, what is interesting is a statement he made about the return from a world cup holiday in Italy. In this statement, he says, that on the return from his holiday with a male friend, he threw a party to celebrate coming home. That night he was plagued with telephone calls from 10 p.m. until 5 a.m. the next day. The caller never gave his name. I was actually questioned about these calls and it was insinuated that I was the harassing caller. Once again another black mark was made in a direct attempt to discredit me.

Prior to this being thrown before me, in conversation under more relaxed circumstances, Carol, had confided to me that on one occasion, Mr Brown and his friend had taken another man with them to a club in Chester, the man in question being a Liverpool footballer, an International player. By accident, it is claimed they found themselves in a gay club. On leaving, the player was accused of overturning a car parked near to the club. Although cleared of this, he was taken to the police station for questioning. Mr Brown happened to keep out of trouble, even though he had been present at the time. Mr Brown I was given to understand had very close ties with the Liverpool club. He is a great supporter, and apparently has entertained players at his home. Again this information comes from Carol. But she had more to tell me about this particular newsworthy player.

Whilst we were still living together, she confided that this player was bothering her, and she was afraid of him. True or not, I fell for her sob story, and she asked me to have a word with him. Next day on my way to the office I called in at Mellwood, the training ground. One of the players went and told the man I wanted to see him. The player came out, a big strapping lad. I asked him to refrain from seeing Carol as we were going through a divorce and she was under a lot of pressure and did not want to be bothered by him. He looked at me coolly and asked who my wife was. I told him and showed him her photograph. He shook his head and said he didn't know her. We exchanged a few words and our dispute closed when the   manager came out and told me to leave. Sadly this action of mine caused my eviction from the family home once again. Carol blew her top when I explained I had been to see the footballer who had been chasing her. She said I should not have gone down there.

Whatever was going on, one thing was clear. I made it easy for Carol to have me ejected. I had acted like the jealous husband, I had been led carefully into a snare. The truth of such an involvement is scant, but I think it is more than likely there was something going on between them. Perhaps Mr Brown had introduced them. He later would prove he didn't mind sharing her with other men.

My ejections had been frequent from the home, but I went back for the sake of the children. When it suited her, Carol didn't mind me being around. I was a useful nanny as well as a loving Dad. But all these small incidents of ejection from the home would eventually be counted against me.

I didn't realise that a brick wall was being built against me, a wall that even my defence would assist in building up brick by brick. Perhaps they never believed in me - perhaps they were inept You decide.

But let us now return to that period prior to my wife leaving our home for good in 1989. Remember now, we were living together but we were going through a divorce. The traumas were on-going, but as always there were quiet patches. The modelling assignments were still coming in, but I now know that half of what she told me was untrue. She used this as an excuse to go off and do as she pleased. Casually she had mentioned a health club where she said she might visit. She said other models went there to get a tan and generally shape up. I took little notice of this. Why should I? I knew if she wanted to go, she would arrange it. She was a free agent as far as I was concerned; all I needed to know was what we would arrange about the boys.

It was a Wednesday in September 1989. I had been at my premises in Kirkby that day, and Carol had prepared a meal for us. The children and I sat down to eat. Carol then said, "I am just nipping down to the shops, I shall only be about thirty minutes or so".

The children and I tucked into our meal and carried on as normal. When we had finished, I tidied up and did the dishes, whilst the children sat in front of the television where I joined them. I looked at the clock and noticed it was going on for quarter past seven. There was no sign of Carol. I thought I would try her mobile phone which she had with her, but there was no answer. I tried a couple of times in the next hour, then I prepared David and Jonathan for bed. Lee went to bed around half past nine and at this point I was becoming quite concerned about Carol. I rang her father after ringing several of her friends, none of whom had any idea where she might be. John drove from the Wirral along with his daughter April, this being some distance from Southport, such was their concern. On their arrival, we again tried her friends in case she had been in touch with them. Still there seemed to be no luck in tracing her. Just after midnight John and April left; he suggested that if I had not heard by morning that I should ring the police. She didn't arrive back and next morning I rang the police.

I told the children mommy had gone on a modelling assignment. I took Jonathan to his nursery school, Lee to his school, David the baby stayed with me. When the police arrived I was dozing off as I had hardly slept the night before.

I was genuinely concerened that something terrible had happened to Carol. I couldn't see how she could possibly leave us all like this. She knew the boys would be so upset without her. My mind puzzled as to who I could contact next. No-one it seemed had any idea where she could be. Why tell me she's going to the shops if she had any intention of staying out all night? None of it made any sense at all; it was also very worrying. I knew I had to contact the police. Carol was still my wife, also the mother of our three boys. I had no other recourse. So what I now tell you is on record with the police.

Two police officers arrived, one male one female. After discussing the situation with them, explaining our divorce, the times my wife had requested the police, in fact the whole story. The police listened and then requested a photograph of Carol. They also asked if I still had her passport. I looked and said yes. They took it. I was totally unaware that she had another passport, possibly more, the same as her false driving licences. The police then made to leave saying that if she contacted me, to let them know. They said she would be reported as a missing person. So she was and this again is on record as a fact of life.

I have to confess, that whilst Carol was missing, I enjoyed a wonderful five days; the children and I visited my sons, and we also went to see Carol's mother, Doris, in Wallasey. There was no dispute between Doris and me and it was all very relaxed. I think by now we realised Carol was just off on some flight of fancy.

On the home front, there was a bright light that helped occupy my mind at this juncture. A potential buyer for the house appeared. So with this and the kiddies to see to, I was busy and glad of it.

On the Monday I collected the children from their schools, and we were sitting at home eating our evening meal when the phone rang. Lee picked it up, and then shouted, "Goody, its mummy". I went over and picked it up. I asked where the hell she had been, and told her the police were looking for her. She told me she had been to a health club in Birmingham, as she just wanted to get away for a few days. She said not to worry about the police as she would call and see them on her way home - which she maintained would be in about two hours.

The children were obviously very excited to see her, and she looked well. She was very brown. I passed a remark about the tan, to which she replied that the sunbeds at the health club were very good; in fact, she said, all the facilities were marvellous.Carol seemed more like her old self, the girl I had fallen for all those years back. She suggested we arrange for a baby sitter and go out for a meal to which I readily agreed. Carol then rang a babysitter we had used before. When she arrived, we took a taxi to the Prince of Wales which in better days we used to frequent for Sunday meals. We enjoyed a lovely meal, had a bottle of champagne and for a short time, it seemed like the old days were back with us. In fact that night we had a long talk, and discussed the future and ended up in bed together, and yes we made love. The next couple of weeks we carried on as if all was well. I like a fool believed her. By October she had started disappearing again to attend modelling assignments.

By now we had a serious purchaser for the house, and a price was agreed. Carol and I again talked things over. This time she told me I could have custody of the children as she wanted to pursue her own modelling career, but this was never to transpire.

****

CHAPTER FIVE
THE LADY VANISHES

A S CHRISTMAS 1989 arrived, we were still in the same house. We had festive decorations. In the porch stood a three foot Santa Claus fitted with a light to illuminate him. In the garden stood a tall Christmas tree decorated with lights, and of course there was one inside too. It looked like any other happy family home at this time of year. There were presents under the tree, and a family Christmas lunch booked at the Prince of Wales. For the children I did my best to make it a happy time. Carol appeared happy enough and we made the best of a bad job. We both knew this was our last Christmas here - the New Year was going to be a new chance for us both.

The rest of the day was predictable, the television was on, the kids played with their toys. To all appearances, we were much the same as any other family. When it became quieter, Carol and I shared a bottle of champagne and then retired.

Next day I rose early and walked our two black miniature poodles, Diddy and Bambi. I must be forgiven for not mentioning them until now but they were lovely little family pets who loved the children. We had had Bambi from a lady named Barbra, and it was she who always looked after them when we were away on holiday. I walked our dogs as I always did each morning. On my return I took up coffee to Carol and planned a day with the children. However, one of the toys I had purchased for Jonathan had a problem. It was a bike. I managed to contact the chap I had purchased it from and he told me he could rectify it. He said I should call down later in the day to his shop and he would correct it or exchange it. At four o'clock I set off with the bike. On my return I was horrified to find no-one in - no Carol, no children. The presents were there, but the house was silent - the tree and the lights looking desolate. It was a very lonely sight and very disconcerting. I looked all over the house, then outside. I just sat there bewildered. I tried ringing her on her vodophone but there was no reply. A million thoughts raced through my head, none of them making any sense. Surely she hadn't gone away with them. Maybe she had popped out to friends, God only knows. Where would I start? I sat there head in hands wondering what to do next. Then the doorbell rang, I jumped up and rushed to open it. It was Lee. He stood there in tears - he was 8 years old, a baby. I pulled him in and hugged him.

"What is it? What's wrong?" I asked him.

Still more he cried. "Mum has left you Dad and sent me home." I held him close. What a sad Christmas memory this would be for him to carry always. At that moment the telephone rang, and I walked over to answer it. It was Carol. She told me she had left me. I was deeply shocked when she said, "Roy said you can have Lee; we can re-educate the other two."

I couldn't believe she really could be that cruel. What a fool I was. I was to discover later that she was staying in a Southport Hotel situated in Bath street, a hotel that she and Roy Brown had used to meet to carry on their affair.

So now she had split the boys apart - an awful thing to do as Lee was very close to Jonathan. Lee was very upset by this sudden shock. But he was unfortunately going to suffer far more than this when his father was later arrested.

Two days before New Years Eve Carol returned with our two boys, telling me she wanted to spend New Year with her family. By family, she meant her parents. I agreed to look after the boys whilst she did so. That night the four of us went to bed around 10.15. About 11.45 p.m. Carol rang to say she was still with her family and that she would return sometime next day to collect David and Jonathan. She then wished Lee and me a Happy New Year. Lee was very upset by this, and so we went downstairs to make some Horlicks and watch the celebrations on television. We then went back to bed. That night by the way the four of us slept in the same big bed. The New Year ahead held little to look forward to for me or Lee, and maybe we both cried hidden tears that night.

Next day, sure enough Carol came to collect the boys. Poor David and Jonathan were upset having to leave again; they loved their Daddy too. Lee again cried as his little brothers and his mother walked away from him yet again. The next weeks were dreadful. Lee and I were very hurt by what had happened.

Carol visited the house frequently over the coming weeks mainly to use the washing machine, and also the sun bed.

Eventually however the house was sold, and then came the next distress. The home was taken apart - everything was to be sold and moved out. Carol arranged for most of this, her friends taking a good deal away. I later discovered that most of the furniture went to Roy Brown's house. One thing I'm sure he'll enjoy is my own personal champagne bucket, and my personal salmon fish cooker which was a present from my own family.

The lounge and dining room fittings went to Carol's sister April. For my part, I arranged to take a furnished house in Formby where Lee and I could live and Lee could continue his schooling in Southport.

I talked the legal position over with my solicitor, Mr Calder, and obtained via the courts an access order enabling Lee and myself time to see David and Jonathan. This was affirmed and at the time it was set that I could have them Saturday from 10 a.m. until 6 p.m. At the time this was acceptable and the arrangement was that Carol would deliver them to her mother's house in Liscard, and I would then collect them and return them there. The situation also was used for other occasions, like the time Carol went to the Grand National with her boyfriend and several footballers.

Carol, I was informed, had now moved into a house on the Wirral. I was not aware that this house was close to Roy Brown's place. I later discovered Carol's sister, Tina, known as Twinkle, a lovely lady, used to look after David and Jonathan throughout Carol and Roy's affair.

Within all this emotional setting I still planned to open the Cherryfields. But really the club was a little too far from the house I had rented, and so my son-in-law, Ray Parker, a Director of his own estate agency business, obtained a house for me in Mersey Avenue in Magull. This was ideal and only several miles from the club. In addition it was convenient for collecting David and Jonathan. I was still very concerned as to how the boys were coping with all this change about them. Carol had proved to be irresponsible and selfish. How could I ever feel they would be safe with her?

It was during this period that Roy Brown went on holiday to watch the World Cup in Italy. Carol staying home to continue her modelling career. While he was abroad, she found time to have a meeting with me in New Brighton where we arranged a meal so that we could have a talk about the children. We also had a meeting in the Cafe Bar in Southport, a place which she and Mr Brown apparently used quite frequently. The very same place where later they would throw a celebration party. What was that celebration? I'll tell you. It was to celebrate my wrongful conviction of attempted murder and seven years' imprisonment. The party was on the very evening of the day of my conviction, a party organised by my ex-wife. It was the talk of Southport, an area where my sons and most of my family lived. I ask you. What had I ever done to deserve that?

At one of our meetings I got the impression Carol had been drinking, as she kept repeating, "Charlie was a good fella."

I just didn't get it. In prison I later discovered that 'Charlie' is a word substitute for a drug. At the time I couldn't make head nor tail of it and I mentioned to her mother that she had been drinking and that I was concerned for David and Jonathan. I also reminded Doris that Carol had not delivered the children to her a couple of weeks back, the excuse being she had taken them to Chester Zoo. The next weekend I arranged to collect David and Jonathan and all seemed fine. She had said I could have them overnight which Lee and I were pleased about. But whilst getting the boys ready for bed, I noticed some large bruising on David's leg; he was also sick several times. The next day when I returned the boys to their grand-mother in Wallasey, I told Doris about the bruises on David's leg, and that he had been sick.

Little did I know that that was to be the very last time I was to see them. I still haven't seen them. I religiously went each week in the hope of seeing the boys but they were never brought there again. Carol refused me the right to see them.

I kept in touch with Doris Grey. I had an old pal who lived near her. Tony used to be a Bingo caller, and so we talked over old times and had a couple of drinks in his local hotel. Lee would be over in his Nan's house, quite happy to stay there until my return from a night out with Tony.

Before we left for home, Doris and I would sit and talk things over about how things were and how David and Jonathan were get-ting on. Sometimes I would get upset about what I heard, other times angry, and yes I did say that Carol and Brown should be ashamed of themselves not letting us see the children. I also said I would take him through every court in the land to embarrass him. I even said he might end up in a wheelchair with broken legs. By this I was referring to the possibility that Carol might do the same to him as she had done to me.

None of this is surprising. I felt frustrated in that I was helpless to do anything about seeing the children. Words were the only things I had and sometimes we all say the wrong ones.

In the end I contacted Mr Calder and explained I was not being allowed to see my boys. I also told him that my meetings with them had been stopped after I had mentioned the bruising on David's leg and the sickness he had been experiencing at the time of the visit. Mr Calder advised me to visit the Child Abuse Centre in Moreton Cross on the Wirral. I did so along with Lee. At the centre we were both interviewed separately and I explained why I had gone there. They said they would make enquiries and look into things for me.

On reflection, I suspect that because I had brought attention to little David and his condition, it was decided I was no longer to have them visit. This move was very cruel to me, and even more so to Lee. I would have thought a solicitor would have known better, he being a divorcee himself. Surely he must have appreciated the importance of letting the children of a split marriage keep in touch with each other.

After this affair, the weeks ran into months and we never heard from Carol or saw her at all. Now it was March, 1990 and Lee said to me, "Dad, I would love to see David and Jonathan." Well considerable time had passed. Surely she would let Lee see the boys if we turned up? It seemed the only answer.

So next morning, Sunday, I drove Lee to the Wirral. I said we would visit his Nan, but on the way call at the address in Greasby his mum had given us weeks before. When we eventually found it, it turned out to be a small close with about eight or ten houses. Lee straight away spotted Carol's car and indicated we should drive closer. I suggested he should jump out and make sure it was her car. Lee did so and came back saying it was and that David's carrycot was in the back. It was about 9.00 o'clock and so I told Lee to go and knock at the door whilst I stayed in the car. I thought Carol might look upon Lee a little kindlier without me there and let him see his   brothers. As I sat there looking at the house, Lee knocked at the door. After a few knocks the bedroom curtains opened and Roy Brown looked out to see who was there. Suddenly someone looked over his shoulder also attempting to look out. I couldn't believe it. It was Carol. My mind fumbled for a few seconds trying to put things in place. My first reaction on seeing

Brown was that we had come to the wrong place, but then there was Carol's car. Before I could think again, there she stood leaning over his shoulder, both of them in a state of undress. I looked up staggered. She was still my wife; the final divorce papers had not been issued or declared, and here was my wife with her solicitor together at a bedroom window. Worse, Lee stood back to look up at the house and he saw them. Lee knocked again, now sure that his mother was in and he could see his brothers, but no one answered the door. Brown and Carol simply moved away from the window, now obviously aware that I was there too. After a few minutes Lee came back to the car.

I told him it was still early and maybe they would get up and come down in a few minutes. But no one came to the door, and I was angry they were treating Lee in this way. Lee hadn't seen his mum or brothers for sometime now. I thought it terrible they should hurt him like this because they didn't want anything to do with me. I told Lee to stay by the car whilst I went to knock at the door. As there was no reply, I called through the letter box.

"Can we please see the children? Just let Lee see them if you don't want me to see them," I called.

Still they ignored us. Lee now became quite upset and the chap next door came out to see what was happening. Seeing Lee in tears, he comforted him and brought him a drink of orange juice. My mind ran from one thought to another. Where were the children?

A couple more neighbours came out to see what was going on. I explained I had brought my son along to see his brothers. I then showed them a photo of the boys and asked if they had seen them around. They said they had not seen them. So where were they? I was puzzled. On seeing a photograph of my wife, one neighbour told me that she was the third woman to have stayed there since he had moved in six months ago. But I wasn't interested in him. I wanted to know where David and Jonathan were.

We waited there two and half hours, and still not one of them came out to speak to me or to Lee. Later they were to report they were afraid of me. If that had been true, why hadn't they rung the police? Surely if we had looked such a threat, the good neighbours would have phoned the police. The truth is they were too ashamed - they both had too much to hide.

We left upset and bewildered. I couldn't forgive them for treating Lee like this. What had he done to them? I put it down to Brown forbidding her seeing him. But on reflection I now see it was a cold-hearted thing to leave Lee out there like that. Her own son, her eldest boy, locked out of her life. How could she do that? It broke Lee's little heart.

But my mind now ran to other thoughts. How long had this affair with Mr Brown been going on? Here was a solicitor acting for my wife in her divorce petition, a man who was directing her in every aspect of her financial affairs and future plans. I couldn't help but think the worst. He was acting not only in her interests but his own too. Perhaps earlier on in their relationship they thought they might share in my insurance claim on the Pavilion fire? If all had been well, they would have claimed fifty percent of my claim. Distraught, these questions ran through my mind. I recalled it was also Mr Brown, through his legal position who had tried to acquire a further active fifty percent in a Bingo club for my wife, actually stated in a letter which a judge was to describe as BLACKMAIL. Yes, it was through him that ALL MY ASSETS HAD BEEN FROZEN. Now he had made sure he had frozen Lee and me out of the lives of David and Jonathan.

It was a cold March day but my heart felt colder. I'd been a fool - I was still being one. But let me ask you this. If I was going to hurt Mr Brown, wouldn't I have done it then? No one would deny I had reason to feel angry, bitter, even hatred. In such a mood, if physical violence was going to happen, surely it would have been then! Well it didn't happen - my anger burnt inside. I went over the day scene by scene. I kept seeing them at that bedroom window, my wife and her boyfriend - my wife and her solicitor.

Yes, I was gutted and as I drove I could see now that the lies I had been told about visiting friends, modelling assignments, and the rest were a ruse to make time for her law man Mr Roy Brown.

When we arrived home, Lee and I said very little at first; we both felt too hurt. I couldn't tell Lee my thoughts. He was far too young. When he did speak, all he wanted to know was - did his mother love him? did his brothers still love him? I comforted Lee and helped him to see that this was just a bad patch we were going through and mummy would come round eventually and things would be better. He bucked up a little and we had a bite to eat. He then went out to play with a pal of his, and the tearing about on their cycles seemed to lift him a bit.

Later in the day I made us a meal and we sat down together to watch the television. I was still very unsettled with what had happened earlier that day. Lee too spoke about it again, both of us still wondering where the boys were since there had been no sign of them in the house at Greasby. I later discovered that they were at a house nearby, a house Carol had rented. Her sister Twinkle had been in the habit of minding them while Carol went round to sleep with Brown.

Sitting there, Lee said he'd like to call his mum. He thought maybe she wasn't well and that's why she hadn't come down to see him. I couldn't say much. He deserved to try. He called Carol on her private vodaphone, for which I was later to receive the phone bill. What a revelation that was! She had made in excess of 40 calls to Mr Brown at his home and office. Some of the calls were as early as 6.30 a.m. - the very time I would be out walking the dogs. Needless to say, I didn't pay that particular account, and it was a lot of money I can tell you.

But getting back to that night and Lee ringing his mother. He got through and Carol spoke to him. He seemed alright about that but then he became upset when Mr Brown spoke to him. I was so angry with what had happened that day that if Mr Brown had been in front of me there and then, I probably would have thumped him, despite all the disadvantages. The fact is I never touched him or attacked him. Neither did I arrange to have a hit man to do the job for me. You are my jury. You are the judge. Two trials and over one million pounds were spent in trying to put the blame at my feet. I was innocent but that didn't stop me getting STITCHED UP.

Sitting there brooding about the call Lee had made, and the way he had been spoken to, I opened a bottle of wine. Lee went upstairs to take a shower and sat watching television in his room. I drank the bottle of wine and opened another. I wanted to blot everything out. I know it was foolish of me but at times like this you do foolish things. I now rang Carol on the vodaphone; it was around ten-thirty. She answered and we had quite a discussion. I told her in no uncertain manner what I thought of her behaviour that day and demanded to know where David and Jonathan were. I also told her I would take him through every court in the land to embarrass him. I said he should be ashamed of himself. At this point I actually heard him laughing in the background. She then rang off switching the phone off so I could not call her again. I drank some more of the wine and rang the number Lee used to ring thinking he was calling his mother. It was of course Brown's number.

I called them twelve times. I was the worse for wear. I was abusive, and I said a lot of things because I was hurt. I wanted to hurt back. It was all verbal but they were recording it. Eventually, depressed and very upset with all that had come out that day, I crawled to bed my sorrows well and truly drowned.

Next day, a Monday, I took Lee to his school in Southport, then went on to Kirkby where I was still endeavouring to re-open the Chrerryfield Social Club. I was experiencing a licensing problem at the time which was eventually resolved. On arriving at the Cherryfield I went to my office as normal and a young lady who was the wife of one of the gentlemen helping me pull the place to-gether, told me there had been several phone calls; there had also been calls for Carol. There had been phone calls for her over the preceding weeks which had not interested me, and neither did these latest calls. However they were later to prove very interesting.

I returned home that evening and Lee and I went over to see Doris Grey. We stayed for a while, then took the poodles down to the beach for a run, after which we returned home.

On the Tuesday I took Lee to school as normal, and then I went on to The Cherryfield where I had a productive day. At 3.00 o'clock, I went to collect Lee from school as usual. As I waited in my car at the school entrance, a tall chap came up to the car and tapped on my window. I lowered it and the man said, "George Armstrong?"

"Yes," I said.

"I have a summons for you issued by Mr Roy Brown. You are to appear in the High Court in Liverpool tomorrow morning," he informed me.

I was shocked. The man went on to explain that it was to obtain a Court injunction forbidding me to contact him or approach his office or his colleagues. In short keep away from him. The last thing in the world I wanted was contact with Mr Brown, or my wife after what had transpired the previous Sunday. I gathered this must be all due to my stupid telephone calls, a very silly move on my part, but hardly the move of a man later to be accused of attempted murder or hiring a hit man!

I rang my solicitor as soon as I could after receiving the summons but he was not available. So next morning I went along to the Crown Court. On arrival I saw a gentleman I knew, a Mr Clive Knight, a Barrister. I explained my reason for being there and he said he would accompany me into court. We had a little wait before we went in as there was a major trial taking place. They were going to slip the injunction in as it was to take only a few minutes. Mr Brown in fact had made sure the injunction was heard by a very eminent High Court Judge; there were also several press people present taking interest in the big trial. They stayed there in the interval when I happened to be called up.

The justice read out the request and instructions that Brown had organised, also the typed transcript of my telephone calls. The judge looked the papers over and made his comments. Mr Brown was not in court; he had sent a barrister friend to present his case. As the judge was going over one or two points, I butted in, and thank God, he let me continue.

"Your honour, does no one tell him off?" I asked.

The judge looked at me bewildered.

"Tell him off? What for?" the judge asked.

"Mr Brown is a divorce solicitor acting for my wife and carrying on an affair with her," I replied. I went on to explain that they had split my family up, and were not allowing us to see the children.

The judge sat there intrigued and listened further as I explained how we had gone to the house we thought was rented by my wife, only to find that it was her solicitor's home. How we saw them at the bedroom window.

The judge stopped me there, and I was lucky to have been allowed to say so much. He then called a clerk to his desk where they spoke in whispers their heads together. When the discussion was ended, the judge sat looking at the papers before addressing me again.

"I appreciate your position and your concern for your children, but you must not go near his home or his office again, or you could be put in prison or heavily fined. Well that was clear enough. I had to stay away from the man. That wasn't a problem. I had no need to see him at all. It was the boys I wanted to see. I wouldn't have gone to the house if I had thought he was going to be there. When the judge finished I couldn't help feeling that he sympathised with me; he had made no comment about the telephone calls and appeared less stern after my own input. He was probably shocked, and let's face it, this was rather a dramatic move Mr Brown had made. I had been angry and upset, I had had no way of venting my thoughts; the telephone was my only link.

When I came outside the press followed me out, wanting to

know the story. I answered truthfully. Two of the men wanted to come to my home and talk with me. I agreed. The paper was the Sunday Sport,and the headline they used was DIVORCE RAT STOLE MY WIFE. I hadn't said this, but in truth I felt little regret that they had called him that. They also printed his address, something I didn't expect, but I was a little naïve in this sort of thing.

So there we were. Lee and I still unable to see David and Jonathan. In fact whenever Lee tried to ask to see them, they happened to be in bed or out playing. They were pushing us further away each day that passed. What really hurts is recently when I made an application to see the boys, and was unsuccessful, Carol said that her home was full of boys. Yes, it would be, because Mr Roy Brown has access to his children. He has them every weekend. His boys play with mine. Lee, now a teenager, still hasn't seen his brothers. Who are they punishing? Lee, David and Jonathan - their cruel barrier has made my children strangers to each other. But what can I expect from two people who knew I was innocent and yet watched me go to prison for a crime I did not commit or instigate.

But returning to that time, I still endeavoured to open my premises in Kirkby. Winter faded; spring came and went; then summer. Still we had not seen or heard from Carol or Roy Brown nor had Lee. They had buried us in the past, but we still had each other, thank God. Lee had started a new school and we were doing the best we could with things as they were.

****

79

The 1950s

Top left: Fighting fit, the future before me.

Top right: The happy family man.

Bottom left: Lil, my first wife, on the town — The Grafton Room, West Derby Road.

CHAPTER SIX
MY ARRESTING BEHAVIOUR

O N THE 17th of August 1990, I arrived home after walking the dogs, turned the radio on and made a cup of tea. I then caught the news that a Merseyside solicitor had been attacked at his home. The bulletin went on to say that the attacker was thought to be a husband of one of his clients. I was curious, so at 8.00 a.m. I listened into the full bulletin. It was Roy Brown. At the time, I remember wondering who it could be - probably a dissatisfied client's husband. After all Mr Brown had shown that he had abused his position with my wife. She obviously would not have been the first. Either way I felt nothing. Certainly not sympathy - it would be a lie to say otherwise.

I got Lee ready for school, drove him there, then went on to Kirkby. On arrival I was greeted by the old cleaner lady who was working the steps of the premises. She asked me if I had heard the news on the radio about the solicitor who had been attacked. Due to the publicity earlier in the year, most people on Merseyside were aware of my connection with Roy Brown. Carol had also been frequently to the premises from October 1989 until the December when she left the house for good. The cleaning lady was the first to mention the plight of Roy Brown, but throughout the day I had numerous calls from people I knew telling me about the attack.

The day went on as normal. I finished at the club, and picked up Lee from school; we arrived home, changed, and went out for an evening meal. Nothing grand I may add; it was our habit to go to the Little Chef restaurant on Northway in Maghull. We had been doing this almost daily as the value was very good and we were able to obtain an excellent meal with a variety of choice. I was aware that Lee, being a growing boy, needed good food for his growth. We would have fish one night, maybe steak another. I always recall my own mother drumming it into me that you grow strong from eating well, or in other words, eat well and you will be well. Being regulars, the staff were very friendly and it made it a nice social occasion for us.

This particular night was the same as most nights - we finished our meal, then went home. Lee played out for a while and I watched television. Within the course of the evening I dislodged a filling in my tooth after chewing several sweets and so I made a mental note to give my dentist a ring next day to have it sorted out.

After walking the dogs, I rang Mr Chu, my dentist and arranged to call in and see him, it was a Saturday and so Lee accompanied me. Mr Chu replaced the filling and Lee and I went on to the Little Chef for lunch, after which we continued on to the club in Kirkby. arriving about midday. I parked my car as normal, this being at the garage opposite my premises. Then we crossed the road. As we did so, two young men in casual clothes, grabbed me by both arms, pushed me across the pavement and up against a large shop window. Next they pinned my arms back. Lee who was only eight years old started screaming, "What are you doing to my Dad?" He was terrified and tried to pull them off me. One of the men pushed him over. I couldn't believe it. Lee and I were in shock. We had no idea who they were, until one of them said,

"George Armstrong?"

I nodded, "Yes.".

They dragged me to the car that had driven up with brakes screaming. Now, other people gathered, many who knew me personally. Several of them came forward to help but they were told "Get back. We are police officers" by one of the men who then showed his identity card. They continued to drag me to the car and pushed me in it. I caught my hand on the top of the car as I fell in. Inside the car, on the back seat were containers. I fell onto these, and poor Lee was then bundled on top of me. One of the young men pushed in beside us. Lee was petrified, and he clung to me for dear life. What a terrible experience for an adult never mind an eight year old child. There was never any call for this treatment; it was unforgivable of them as they acted like thugs. Then the car drove off at high speed, once again tyres screeching. When we arrived at Kirkby police station which was nearby, and so I don't know what all the dash was about, we were taken inside. Yes, Lee too. I personally knew several officers who were in the reception area, men that had visited The Cherryfields whilst conversion was taking place.

Again I was dragged across the reception area, my son still crying and calling out "Leave my Dad alone, leave him alone."

I was taken to the desk, my arms still held behind my back. The three young plain clothes officers spoke to the officer on the desk. He turned round and wrote on a large board behind the desk: GEORGE ARMSTRONG: ATTEMPTED MURDER.

I was shocked beyond belief. Me George Armstrong - charged with murder. It was a nightmare! How could any of this be true?

I looked around and saw the faces of other people, civilians. They could read it too. I was stunned as the men emptied my pockets as I was pushed closer to the counter desk. Then I was dragged to an empty room and shoved in. Lee was taken to another room by a lady, still screaming. Inside I too was screaming. I'm still screaming. This should never have happened to me. It most definitely should never have happened to Lee. He still remembers that terrible day, and he always will. He will carry that scar for the rest of his life.

I was held in the room until another man arrived. The two men then told me I had been arrested for the attempted murder of Roy Brown, the solicitor. They said he had been attacked at 6 a.m. the previous day at Greasby. I was in too much of a state to think straight, and so it never occurred to me at the time to ask why they had waited over thirty hours before coming for me? Why indeed?.

Carol knew where I could be found, as did Roy Brown. So why was it left so long? Personally I think it was because Brown suspected it was an acquaintance of his. But I was convenient, I was the betrayed husband, and it was easy to point the finger at me.

Eventually, after being questioned in depth, the police gave me a cup of tea. I kept on telling them they had made a terrible mistake. Why on earth would I want to murder Roy Brown? As much as I disliked the man, the thought had never entered my head. Yes, I could have punched his nose for taking up with Carol and splitting the children apart, but this was crazy and I'm not a crazy man. This was horrendous.

The officers informed me that they wanted to search my club premises. So off we went, Lee with us. Whilst Lee and I sat in my office with two officers, other officers searched the club, but they didn't say what they were looking for. They piled items of clothing, documents and put them all in a bin liner. The documents and diaries I never saw again. They also took the keys to a hire car I was using - my own car was having repairs completed at the garage. Items from the car were also taken. When they had done, they said they wanted to go to my home. We then moved on to Mersey Avenue in Maghull. All the time I was thinking, this will stop soon. How can they be doing all this? I'm innocent. But the madness had only just begun. When we reached home, Lee and I were kept in the lounge whilst other officers searched the house. Again items were brought in and pushed into the bin liner. Even the contents of waste and rubbish bins were turned over in an effort to find something against me. Lee was now allowed to take the dogs for a walk whilst the officers persisted in questioning me about the attack on Brown. I told them that I honestly knew nothing about it, but this didn't stop them repeating their accusations. I felt under a great strain and wondered how long it was going to take before they found the real attacker.

On Lee's return, the police took us back to the police station. On the way, I noticed Mrs Smith who worked for me, outside my club. I asked the police if we could stop and tell her what had happened and they agreed. We stopped and I gave her the keys to the club and said we wouldn't be long, explaining what had transpired. One of the officers agreed we wouldn't be long. Mrs Smith, seeing how distraught Lee was, insisted they let Lee go with her. She had heard what had happened to me and was very angry with the police. She virtually pulled Lee from the car. I'm very grateful she did, for I had more to face. Mrs Smith had become a good friend over the months of organising the club; she had looked after Lee many times, now and then giving him meals while the alterations were taking place. So I knew he was in safe hands.

The police, surprised by Mrs Smith's determination, let Lee go with her. Little did Lee and I know that Mrs Smith and her family would be home to Lee for two years and five months. For the wheels had started to roll and the circus was about to take me to town.

Once at the station, I was met by two Inspectors who had arrived from the Wirral. I was told I was being taken to Birkenhead Police station. I was escorted to their car park where their car and driver awaited. At Birkenhead, the Police station adjoins the court. This was all getting out of hand. I continued to plead my innocence, but my words fell on deaf ears. As far as they were concerned, I was guilty. Once inside the station, I was taken down to the cells, and locked in a filthy cell that had obviously just been vacated. The place stank, and on the floor were strewn torn up newspapers. There was a mattress with two blankets on the floor and in a closet there was a urinal bucket that was full to the brim with spew and crap. I stood in this hell hole and looked up to the small window eight feet from the ground. How could this be happening? How could they get things so wrong? Why was I being treated like this? I felt like a condemned man and being put in this disgusting cell was nothing short of criminal. I spent two days in this cell before being brought up to the court rooms above. I was smelly, dirty and unshaven. I pride myself on my cleanliness and appearance; feeling ashamed like this was abhorrent to me. In retrospect I now see this treatment was part of their tactics to break me down, to make me confess to a crime I had not committed. On the first night, Saturday, I was taken up to the station and met by the officer in charge, Inspector Dorkins who asked me if I wanted a solicitor. Since it was now Saturday night who on earth could I get? I couldn't remember the telephone number of my own solicitor, Mr Naylor or Mr Calder. But at this time I was still of the mind that soon it would all be over and I would be allowed to go home. The Inspector suggested I have the duty solicitor, and I agreed as I needed someone on my side right at that moment. They took me back to the stinking cell which had a small low light bulb for comfort. I sat there and became very distressed. I broke down as I thought of Lee, then of my dogs who had been locked up in the house all day with no-one to tend to them. It was gone nine now, the night was coming on fast and there was no sign of my release. How much more of this could I take? I wasn't a young man. I was sixty one for God's sake. I hammered on the door, my frustration coated with panic and anger. A policeman shouted to me through a small hole "What do you want?"

"Can I use a phone please?" I asked.

He said he would enquire. Ten minutes later he returned and said I could. He led me to the ground floor where there was a telephone on the wall. I rang my brother Lawrence and told him what had happened. He was very shocked and said he would be over to me straight away, and true to his word he was. But the police refused to let him see me. Lawrence then left and went and picked up the two poodles from my home and took them over to Mrs Smith who was looking after Lee.

Meanwhile, I was again taken from the cell to an office in the station. There I sat with Inspector Dorkins and the solicitor who after hearing what it was about said he couldn't represent me as he was a personal friend of Mr Brown. He advised he would get another solicitor from Chester to come and see me later that night.

I could hardly believe my ears. I stood there taking blow upon mental blow. I was in a terrible state by now and began to feel ill with it all. Again I was marched down to my nightmare cell. I had been given one cup of tea all day, nothing to eat. Not that I think I could have eaten, but again I now feel it was all power to their cause, pushing me to a point where I would say anything to get out of there.

At about 11 p.m. the next solicitor arrived - a Mr Alexander, who like a ministering angel helped and guided me through the next several hours of questioning. Mr Alexander informed me of the procedure that was to commence, and told me that everything would be recorded. I asked him if all the other accusations and insinuations had been recorded. He said NO. Again I WONDERED WHY ?

Prior to Mr Alexander's arrival, the two Inspectors had accused me of arranging the assault on Brown, and that I would be given eight years in prison for it. They told me they were convinced I had either committed this terrible crime or arranged to have it committed. Now with the solicitor present their attitude changed. They set up the recording equipment and proceeded with their questioning. I completely denied the charges made against me, and protested my innocence quite clearly. As the interview, or should I say interrogation, went on, the name of Doris Grey was mentioned. I could see the police were staggered to hear she still lived as my now ex-wife Carol had told them she was dead. But why? But then this was only one small absurd lie she had told. How many more greater lies had been told and were about to be told? Many - many, I can assure you. The lies now started to breed like flies, Brown hiding his in a cloak of silence which eventually would be uncovered.

The two Inspectors continued to question me in the presence of Mr Alexander, the second tape running out around midnight when the officers sealed the tapes, and I together with Mr Alexander signed to the fact they were sealed. It was arranged we would meet at 10.30 a.m. Sunday morning. The officer informed me I would be kept overnight in the cells. I strongly objected, as did Mr Alexander. I explained that my son would be distraught, and my little dogs needed to be attended to. I pleaded my innocence again, stressing I hadn't done anything. To no avail. I was returned to my filthy cell and locked up for another night in dire squalor. I was exhausted and in a state of shock. I could take no more. I crumbled in a heap and just sat there crying my eyes out. I couldn't sleep, my mind worrying over Lee, that poor little lad of mine left alone and confused by all this. He was being punished just as much as me, and for what? I hadn't done this crime they had accused me of, nor had I been involved in anything so bizarre as hiring a hit man. Someone's dream of events had created a nightmare for me, a nightmare that I will never awake from, not fully. I was mentally and emotionally tortured and so was Lee. It was unforgivable and the people who did this to me never really knew me if they thought I would simply lie down and die.

At around 6.30 a.m. a police officer came into my cell. I was not aware of time as they had removed all my belongings. But he told me the time and allowed me to have a cup of tea. He said I would get breakfast at 8.30 a.m. which I did. I then asked if I could wash and shave. He shook his head No shave, but yes, I could wash. This was to be the first morning I had never shaved, and I felt a mess. Surely it wouldn't have hurt to let me shave? But then I can only think someone wanted me to look rough, very rough.

I was left in my cell locked up until about 10.30 a.m. I was taken back to the office for another interview, but as I was being escorted there by the officer, we were both stopped by Inspector Ivor Dorkins. The Inspector said,

"We have arrested two people."

I looked at him and said "Oh good, can I go home now?"

Strangely, the Inspector smirked and said "We have got the right man."

I was amazed at this comment as it was clear he meant me. He had already made up his mind I was the man. I only wish he had made the remark in the presence of my solicitor, but of course these words were for my ears alone. It was another one of his tactics to put the fear of God in me. When we were settled in the interview room, and my solicitor Mr Alexander arrived, I mentioned to him that the inspector had said they had two people they were questioning. So again I asked the inspector if I could I go. His reply was to the effect that 'we would see'. Quite different you will notice to his earlier remark. After this, the tape machine was started and the questioning lasted all day. They used about six tapes and recorded all aspects of my knowledge of Mr Brown and my relationship with my wife Carol. Throughout the questioning, I completely denied any knowledge or involvement in this attack on Mr Brown, and this can be borne out with all my statements I made at this time.

It was during this particular questioning that they played my stupid phone calls to Carol and Brown, twelve in all. The calls had been made five months previously after that fateful day when Lee and I had gone over to try and see the children. That cold March day 1990, when Carol and Roy Brown had stood at the bedroom window in a state of undress, the day they ignored my son's plea to open the door.

Yes, they were stupid calls, they were from someone hurt, angry and drunk. I said some foolish things, including one that, if they thought I was too old, I would get my brother to punch him on the nose. But in the main the calls were nothing more than a vent to my frustration. I criticised them, and I said I would take them through every court in the land.

Then the Inspector played another recording from a man saying,

"BROWN, I HAVE THE CONTRACT ON YOU. I'M GONNA FUCKING WRAP YOU UP FOR GOOD.

The Inspector then questioned me regarding that particular phone call. As my statement proves, my answer was simply, "I haven't a clue".

The Inspector then said, and it was recorded.

"I am of the belief that you arranged this contract that is referred to on one of those tapes. I think you're behind it."

To which I denied all knowledge. I didn't even recognise the voice, let alone know who it was.

Months later, at my trial a cassette would be brought into court and played there for all to hear. A tape the jury would listen to several times. That recording now featured my calls made in March and the May contract threat. The Inspector actually had both the cassettes edited on to one cassette in a bid to link me with the mystery caller. I still maintain that was tampering with evidence, as the cassette heard in court was a doctored version.

But back there being questioned, I never dreamt this crazy business could go so far.

On hearing the contract threat again, I denied all knowledge or association with this person.

I now know that this threatening call was made on the 24th of May 1990. Mr Brown had gone along to Hoylake Police station the following evening to report the call. They also told the police who they believed it to be. The name they gave was Terry Lyed, Carol's brother-in-law, with whom she had formed a close liaison at some time in the past. This fact would later come to light when her sister disclosed their association to me. However, at that point in time I was completely in the dark about it. At about 4 p.m. the officers concluded their interview with me, and escorted me to the desk near the cells and formally charged me.

The officers allowed me two minutes alone with Mr Alexander, who informed me what would happen next. He told me I would appear in court the following morning, a Monday. He commented that from what he had heard throughout my questioning, I had nothing to worry about and he would contact Mr and Mrs Smith, who had taken in Lee along with my dogs. Also that I was coping and should be back home tomorrow after the Magistrates' hearing. This eased me a little, but I was soon back in the hell of my stinking cell. They wouldn't even let me clean the filthy place, and so the toilet area remained intolerable. I had not shaven for two days, my clothes and shirt were a mess, I was ashamed of my appearance and felt low on self respect. But then that is how they wanted me to feel and look. No man should be allowed to experience the trauma and treatment that I received whilst being held like this. And poor Lee, mentally scarred for the rest of his life. For what? Because they suspected me of a crime? No, because they were sure it was me. But who had put that lie on my shoulders? Yes, Mr Brown and his wife to be. I was always innocent, but take it from me, being innocent is no protection from lies and conspiracy. I had to start fighting for the TRUTH.

At the time, the lies swept over me like an ocean, the newspapers tolled my conviction bell constantly. Not once did they ask for my side of the story. This campaign went on before, throughout, and after my trial. In 1992 *Bella* magazine gave Mr and Mrs Roy Brown a two page photo interview that was in their February 4th publication - Issue 4. There my ex -wife still continued to tell lies, plenty of them. She claimed that she was my accountant! Quite a fancy name for a barmaid! But then they were being paid for this fantasy article. Why not improve by degrees? Nothing could stop them it seemed. They loved the press. They played their sad song before my second trial, and they laboured it again when my appeal came up. Now in 1995, they have moved to the television, appearing on the Channel 4 programme *Cutting Edge*, Monday the 30th of January. *Revenge* was the title, and once again they slurred my name, even though my sentence was quashed. In the programme, they are called 'The Lovers' but really it should have read 'The Liars.'

As the conspiracy against me grew, I questioned the power of the old school tie, or was it perhaps a secret society I was up against? Paranoia is a shadow you can't shake off when you feel persecuted in this way. It has to be said that there were some dirty tricks going on within all matters concerning my arrest and the legal procedures. It is only natural that I questioned the possibility that there was some secret society operating. Let's face it, the law and the legal fraternity does have a reputation for membership to closed societies.

Read what Judge Pickles said in the *Sun* newspaper, November 10th 1993.

"Hero of the week is Labour M.P. Chris Mullen for sponsoring a Bill to make M.P.s, Judges, and Barristers, and other legal people declare membership of these secret societies." He says, "I am not a Freemason, but many Judges and Barristers are. It helps them get on in the law; there is no other sensible reason for bearing the breast or roll up a trouser leg - kids' stuff, but it can have sinister side effects."

Sinister is the word. What has happened to me has happened under very sinister circumstances. There is a web of deceit here so intricately woven that the liars cannot go back and look the truth in the eye. They know it will blind them. Still the magic and mystery goes on.

Chris Mullen failed to get his Bill passed. Are you surprised? I'm not.

In the future, I would have plenty of time to think of this and many other things. For my coffin had been made and measured for me, and I was far too blind and scared to face it. The pressure was laid on as systematically they tried to break me down.

On the Monday, the day before the hearing, a man came up to me, and remember I was locked up in a cell in the annexe of Birkenhead Magistrates Court. He said, "I am the local probation officer, and I just want to advise you that during today's hearing, if you wish to make a comment regarding your involvement with the happenings to Mr Brown, you may, and, if it assists the police to catch this attempted murderer, you could be admonished with a severe dressing down. On the other hand, you could end up with 10 to 12 years' imprisonment - it's up to you. This is good advice."

I am now convinced, that this was another dirty trick played by Inspector Dorkins. He hoped I would be coaxed into incriminating myself, and thereby support this supposed jealousy motive they had come up with. They got short change from me. I was far too shocked with it all even to reply.

Next day my case was heard in the presence of undisguised hostility. The film already loaded, the cameras and keyboards were set to roll on their latest news story. The one about the jealous husband who hired a HIT MAN.

Read what Mr Alexander, the solicitor who attended the-interview with me, - you know, the solicitor that had to come up from Chester because the duty solicitor was a friend of Mr Brown's - had to say:

30th of August 1990

From: Clive J Alexander, Solicitors Upper Northgate, Chester.

Dear George,

I am sorry I was not able to see you after the hearing on Tuesday, but the door to the cells was locked again and the bus had just left for Walton Jail and they refused me access to you.

I felt very, very angry at the refusal of the bail application and extremely concerned regarding your predicament.

The atmosphere in the court fairly bristled with local feelings and prejudice in the very literal sense of the word and I would not blame you for thinking that a negro in Alabama U.S.A in 1950 would have had a better chance of justice. I have never before sensed this degree of antipathy in any court for some time.

I will attend court myself personally rather than rely on a barrister, just in case this Dorkins tries more of his cheap tricks like the stupid Mike Whitewash trick he pulled last time.

I should have stayed in the charge of Mr Alexander. I made a very big mistake by not doing so. But I had been approached by Mr Red, a solicitor's clerk who was involved with the solicitors Castle and Castle of Liverpool. They approached me suggesting they take over my case and application for bail. I had known Mr Red for a number of years in a social way. Unknown to me then, and for reasons best known to himself, Mr Red was not employed by these solicitors.

Mr Red turned out to be of more use to my prosecution than to me. He made a complete mess of the thorough and truthful evidence which was given to him. Failing to pass this information on, he obtained monies from my sons and family to obtain, he claimed, application for bail, one of which was made in the London High Courts. On this occasion the barrister failed to turn up! But nevertheless the money was claimed for. Who the hell made the application that day? Was it another member of a secret circle? Either way, it was refused for the fourth time.

Still Mr Alexander gave me his support. How foolish I was, not to have stayed with his counsel. Read what he said expressing his dismay at the result of the application for bail that he made on my behalf.

This nightmare must be unbearable for you, especially being separated from your son Lee, who I am told is standing by his Dad all the way. I can assure you George that no stone will be left unturned in efforts to restore you to each other's company. I promise.

I now feel sure that if I had continued with Mr Alexander, I would not have been convicted of a crime I was never guilty of.

After my appearance in the Birkenhead Magistrates' Court, I was remanded into custody, then taken by a Black Maria lock-up van to Walton jail. On the journey we actually passed by the Princess Bingo Club. Through the tiny window in the partition, I could see members going into the building. My heart sank and I broke down once again. How on earth could this be happening to me? What the hell was going on? I was trapped and alone as the van moved onwards to its destination.

Soon we were at the two large prison gates of Walton Jail. Thank God I hadn't accepted that this was going to be my home for the next eight harrowing months. Still handcuffed I was taken into the reception area. My pockets were searched and I was told to strip naked. I was shocked and humiliated beyond belief. Here we all stood, being processed as they called it. Men who were to be locked up for various crimes. Then we were ordered to take a shower. From there with nothing more than a small towel, we marched to a store where I was issued with clothes that were far too big for me, and a pair of boots. My own clothes were packed into a container and put away. Next we were taken in line to an office-where we were examined by a doctor.

He asked me many questions. Did I take drugs? Was I feeling suicidal and did I need to take a hospital cell. I said No to the hospital cell, but later I was to end up in there for a time due to illness brought on by the shock of it all, the stress, the sheer hell of being there. I could have so easily died in prison, and maybe that is what some people wanted to happen. But I had too much to fight for, and Lee was out there.

After the interview with the doctor, me and another prisoner were taken to another part of the prison. This involved being escorted through various wings as they were known, which held five landings. I was placed in a cell on my own on the ground floor of B wing. I was given some bedding and locked into the cell. Once again I broke down, wretched and weak at what the day had brought me. A little later one of the officers came along and gave me a mug of tea and a sandwich. Assisting the officer there was a prisoner who was to become a firm friend as the days passed by. He told me at a later time that he had been on remand a long time in B Wing. He was on a murder charge, for which he was later found guilty. Because this particular prisoner had read all about my case in the newspapers, he had locked onto the idea I really had hired a hit man. He indicated that others in the prison thought I had Mafia connections. I did my best to try and convince him this was ludicrous, but then these people wanted to believe this myth. For my part it probably kept some of them off my back. So maybe it was a blessing in disguise.

****

95

CHAPTER SEVEN
PRISONER OF LOVE

MY first night was torture. I couldn't sleep. Mice were running around the cell floor, and because B wing was situated in a basement, over the next months I would have many encounters with mice and rats. But that first night was appalling. My thoughts were all for Lee, and the good people who had taken Lee home with them. Mr and Mrs Smith and their daughter June had assured me they would look after him regardless of my situation, and I am eternally grateful for their kindness to both of us. The trauma was to affect Lee terribly, for many weeks after our separation. What in justice they had meted out to me had punished Lee in its wake. They had torn us apart, and shackled Lee in his own dark cell of fear. A cruel fate for an eight year old boy - a day can be a lifetime to a child. How could he ever believe he would see his Dad again?

On my first morning in Walton Jail, I was allowed to queue with other prisoners for breakfast, that being porridge, toast and sausage with a mug of tea. You then took it on your tray to your cell. I was still ashamed of my scruffy appearance. The prisoner who I had spoken to the night before managed to slide a mirror and razor under my door, and so whilst slopping out, I managed to get some water in my bucket. The bucket ritual was due to the fact that this was the only available sanitation in your cell on B wing.

So I managed to clean myself up a little and restore a small essence of some dignity in my shattered soul.

Next came the interview with the Deputy Governor who informed me about the amenities and the rules regarding visits. Also, because I was over sixty, I would be put into a cell on landing No. 2. This would mean that I wouldn't have to climb. I would also be given a job as a cleaner, which would allow me a little time out of my cell during the period I was on remand.

I could not allow my son Lee to come and visit me in Walton Jail for I knew it would have broken his heart even more to see his Dad in these awful circumstances. I loved him too much to put him through that, as much as my heart ached to see him.

On my third day in Walton, I was placed in a cell with another prisoner and began an existence which I find hard to recount. We were locked up for 23 hours a day .

My position of cleaner did give me a little extra freedom, if you can call it that. It was in fact 45 minutes when I was allowed to sweep and mop out a toilet area on the same landing as my cell.

The same morning I was to meet a jovial character by the name of Timmy, also awaiting trial. Timmy, it turned out, was Acting Supervisor, along with a Prison Warden, in arranging various prisoners to assist in the serving of food at meal times. Later I would be chosen to assist on this duty, again giving me more free time out of my cell.

During the whole of my remand period, I was moved about six times. Six different cells, and within those moves I was to witness many, many incidents which involved other prisoners having disputes over cigarettes and other various dealings that go on in these places. I have to admit that the prison officers have to do a hell of a job and I do sympathise with their lot. They deal with some really bad characters. So it was no surprise that I did become friendly with one or two of these officers. In one conversation it came out that several officers knew Mr Roy Brown - in fact he visited Walton on many occasions. The company he worked for

Smethers Warpole and Smethers even represented the Prison Officers' Association. So it seemed the connection still went on, and Roy Brown and Carol were still on my case. In fact the officers knowing the case well, made me quite a well-known prisoner amongst them. Once they got to know me, I feel many of them believed my innocence, but it made life no less harrowing in those dark days.

My solicitor, Mr Red, visited me several times. With him came the barristers Mr White and Mr Knight who were to represent me at the Crown Courts in Liverpool.

Lil also came to see me with sons Gary and Mark. This meant a great deal to me; I didn't deserve such love and loyalty from them.

Also my brother Lawrence visited me, and on one occasion he brought along Mrs Lyed, the sister of my wife Carol who told me she was ashamed of her sister's behaviour prior to the attack on Roy Brown. She also told me who had made the stupid contract threat to Roy Brown. She said it was her ex-husband Terry Lyed. A point that would be later confirmed by several people. Perhaps it was a silly prank of a call or something more vicious? Who knows? One thing I do know is that it was that call, recorded by Mr Brown in May 1990, that was produced in August 1990 by Inspector Dorkins at my trial and used as evidence against me. What is beyond all reason is the fact that the Inspector, Carol and Roy Brown knew the police had been informed as to who Roy Brown thought the caller to be.

Still Inspector Dorkins used this tape with the Prosecution and conspired to convince the jury that I had hired a contract killer.

But right now all I had was the cold comfort of Walton Jail, and my trial had now been set for February 1991 when I would come before Judge Crowe at the Liverpool High Crown Court. So now I knew. I had to face all those months away from Lee, and with no possible chance of seeing David and Jonathan.

The strain now started to tell on me, and my son Gary arranged privately for a doctor - a heart specialist from Broadgreen Hospital - to come and examine me. I had not been well for a while and I began to suffer with chest pains. The Deputy doctor had prescribed Algipan rubbing ointment and locked me in a hospital cell. I became so ill on remand that my visits to the hospital cell were frequent. In fact I lost 1½ stone in weight through this bad time. When I did see the heart specialist, it came out that my heart had swollen a little and that I needed to take care. Swollen! My heart was ready to burst open. There were times when I thought I would never see the trial; I thought body and soul would never make it. But Lee and my family who comforted me kept me alive.

The majority of the prison officers were very considerate to me. They showed understanding and treated me well, and there wasn't anything privileged about this; they just showed some leniency, because after all I wasn't a young man.

There were okay prisoners too who all seemed to know about my lot. I suppose I had some kind of celebrity status, none of which I wanted or encouraged. There were the hard cases too. I even had one man offer to be a hit man for me, a young Irish lad. He was quite serious too, and he took a lot of persuading that I did not want that kind of help thank you. The Hit Man offer - a more detailed kind - was to come again from another source, but I will tell you about that later.

It was now Christmas 1990. This was a terrible time. I was not allowed to speak to Lee, and my only contact was by letter. I was heartbroken about this and I know he was too. Lee means the world to me; I would be lost without him for he is my world. But our world had fallen to pieces, and we both were hanging by threads. Thankfully the strong threads of love.

I recalled all those happier days when I had been with my children. The laughter I had known. The trappings of a good life, a very good life that had been won honestly. I had striven, worked and found success. How on God's earth could I be here in Walton jail living in such harsh conditions? Here, locked up with criminals, strange people, professional and perpetual law breakers.

It was madness, and you had to hold on to faith of some kind to keep going. The things I would experience were beyond all comprehension. There were three suicides that took place in the term of my incarceration there. The one body I witnessed being carried in a black sealed bag from landing 4. He was a young man I was told. The method of death all three had used was hanging. They did this by placing their table below the window which was 7ft from the floor, the window being about 2ft diameter. They would then attach a piece of material to the steel window frame, then around their neck, then they would kick away the table until death came to them. All three suicides took place at night, at a time when only a duty official would be in charge of the wing. So the night had its own special darkness, a time when those locked up felt the darkness closing in on them, suffocating their reason, and letting their   personal demons come to haunt them.   Suicide was always the last option of the night. Guilty or innocent it was a route so many must consider in times like this.

The officers had locked all prisoners safely up for the night, their tour of duty finishing after the evening meal and slop out. After the tea at 6.o'clock, a prisoner was not allowed out of his cell apart from the exercise period of 30 minutes a day, plus queueing for meals.

Because I was a well-behaved prisoner, I was given the privilege of being allowed to empty the wing bins. I was one of a company of about ten prisoners, and we were escorted by three officers. This meant that each day we would physically carry the bins to the refuse area which was in the prison walls near to the exercise area. Next to that was another section fenced off by a 20ft steel mesh through which was H Wing, where all the sex offenders were kept. From where we stood we could see their exercise area and the prisoners with me would often shout abuse at the men. But then those men deserved it - they were men who had abused or attacked children and they were despised by us all.

101

I did meet some good individuals whilst serving my time. Really solid people, not all the men there were thugs and murderers. There were men from all walks of life, men that were in trouble for the first time; possibly some of them should never have been there at all. Perhaps like me, they had found themselves in there by some odd turn of fate. For our part, we had the hope that justice would be done and we very soon would see the outside world again.

For now me and my fellow prisoner would take it in turns to look out on our limited small world. We could see very little, but hope always has new buds, and when you are locked up for so many hours, even a peek at very little is something. Some prisoners on the upper floors could even observe a glimpse of the outside world; they were lucky.

Another duty I was given at Walton was serving the bread. I was instructed to give each individual two pieces only, and that is what I did. But on one occasion a strange inmate took it in his head to take the two slices and several more. I did no more than snatch them back. The man went totally berserk - he threw his tray at me, and his mug, threatened to beat me up, and all manner of things. It was only when the prison officers intervened that he calmed down and backed off. After that I became a joke amongst the officers, and I was told never to stop any of the men from taking extras. They explained that at the end of the line one of the officers would have retrieved the extra portions. I was lucky that time, and nearly learned the hard way what not to do.

I was also to learn various ways of breaking the law, and I was also instructed in how I could make a lot of money. I would never take advantage of this schooling, but one method was related by a man whom I will call Cliff. Cliff was a clever man who was in prison for making a lot of money, millions in fact. He had done this by fraud involving banks. But then there were so many tutors in the art of crime on hand. Many only too eager you should take advantage of their expertise, and so I always listened attentively, even though I never had any intention of breaking the law. As the learning was offered, the friendships secured, and enemies ignored, my time on remand moved forward.

February was now only weeks away. The trial loomed before me. I knew that my defence must get everything right. I was innocent, but I knew by now that that wasn't enough. I really had to prove it. Carol and Roy were still peddling their sad story of how I had tried to destroy them; in fact it is fair to say that press-wise, I was hung, drawn and quartered before I ever saw the dock.

But now came another visit from my legal people. Mr Red, a solicitor's clerk at the time, Mr Knight a barrister and Mr White. Mr Knight was a marvellous gentleman, and if he had been representing me, he would have wiped the floor with the ridiculous suggestions put forward by the prosecution. But that was not to be as you will discover.

During this period prior to my first trial, I compiled numerous pieces of evidence which I obtained with the help of Mr and Mrs Smith. This had been accumulated during the visits made by them and my family. The evidence I had collated was overwhelming. I also could bring forward witnesses. Sadly most of it would never come to light at either of my trials as none of this evidence would be produced. Nor were any of the witnesses called on my behalf.

I am now convinced beyond a shadow of doubt that the first trial would never have taken place if that evidence had been put forward and the witnesses disclosed, prior to the trial. Incredibly, the documentation I had with all this information was borrowed and I foolishly let it out of my protection. Along with that information were police statements against me, and reading these would have been amusing if it all hadn't been so very serious. They were full of contradictions and lies. Arthur who we shall call my cell mate read these and marked the contradictions with a coloured pen to highlight them. When I handed them to Mr Red, he studied them and appeared staggered at the obvious errors in the statements. All had been signed and sworn, but any professional man could spot those errors, as Arthur had in Walton Jail. Mr Red then asked if he could borrow them. Well as he was on my side, it seemed reasonable to let him have them, and so I did. But then something strange happened once they were in his charge. They all went missing!

Later I was to discover all the documents had been destroyed, including the statements against me. Why? Because the prosecution evidence they had was proven to be concocted. To avoid this embarrassment coming out, they were lost for a while in the system. In the meantime I was to lose any hope of a fair trial.

The Police, covering their back, now blame the prosecution for my WRONGFUL CONVICTION. They have in fact several times, and quite recently, suggested I take out action against the Prosecution. But the police are not blameless in this, as I have told them on a number of occasions. They would not have had a case if it had not been for the evidence they put forward - evidence created (lies) and the magic hit man tape.

But now the time had come for my trial. Many people wished me well, both prisoners and officers. In fact on several occasions, a comment had been made that always gave me some hope. Someone would say, "You would be surprised George at the number of prison officials who believe you're innocent."

With all the bad things that had happened there, and there were many incidents, even some amusing ones, it was good to feel others believed me. I had also been treated a little kinder perhaps because of my age. Either way I was praying I would soon be free and seeing Lee again.

At 7 a.m. I was taken down to the reception area of Walton Jail and given back the clothes that I had arrived in all those months ago. I looked at them, my only connection to the world outside. When I put them on I felt tearful; they were creased and worse for wear just like me. They now hung on me because of my weight loss, and with the close haircut I had been given the day before, I felt awful. I felt ashamed of what I must look like, and how I would appear in the court. What would my poor family think of me? Thankfully, that week my brother arranged for me to have a clean shirt and tie, and another suit, and this helped a little to brave it all.

So now the journey began to the court. I was one of about 15 other prisoners to board the coach. Handcuffed, I sat there in the hope that now things would come right, and justice would be done. The coach moved on and I looked around at a world I had been locked away from. Emotion trembled inside me; all those months had knocked me about. I was not the same man that had been taken there all those months ago. Who could ever be the same after such an ordeal? For the next two weeks I was to be transported to and from the Crown Courts, and every day the vehicle passed the Princess Bingo Club - my true Princess that had helped give me a life so very different from the one I had now.

The first day was taken up with legal arrangements, points of law and other matters regarding the selection of the jury. But during the first day, an incident happened which I know now was a distasteful dirty trick by my wife Carol and her husband-to-be. They walked into the court together and sat on the front bench, only ten yards from where I sat with a prison officer on either side of me. They did no more than clasp hands and place their hands on the bench so that I could clearly see this, then stared at me. One of the officers with me leant over and said, "Ignore them George - they are trying to wind you up." I realised later that Brown was hoping I would jump up and demonstrate in some way, but I completely ignored them and was honestly not concerned. But of course this display was not only for me, it was for their press. THE VICTIMS, THE LOVERS had become hooked on publicity, any publicity. Little did the press realise that I too was A VICTIM.

But let me take you back into the court on that first day. Several of my relations had turned up, also Mr and Mrs Smith who had now been caring for Lee all those months. His mother, one of THE LOVERS, had not bothered to contact Lee or see him in all this time. She had in fact completely disowned him. I think that speaks volumes about her, and points to a coldness and detachment. But then she had shown that detachment when she went away for several days leaving the boys with me, "JUST NIPPING DOWN THE SHOPS," she said. Tell me this dear reader - if I was such a danger, if I had hit her and did all the things she claimed I did, why then did she feel safe enough to leave the three boys with me? I toll you why. Because she knew I wouldn't hurt them, and she knew I wouldn't hurt her.

So there they sat, a couple who thought they would get half a million pounds from the insurance claim on the Pavilion, the couple who had frozen my assets and tried, via blackmail, to obtain a share in my new business.

But still I was the one on trial. Here I stood charged with a crime I had not committed. What strange madness possessed them that they could want me punished like this? And what about the real attacker? He was still out there.

The jury were sworn in and the trial began. The Judge was Lord Justice Crowe, a prominent man with a reputation for being fair, but if you were found guilty he was severe.

The charges were read out, the first charge being that I was charged with assaulting Mike Whitewash, Carol's cousin. Well I told you all about that earlier. But now it seemed the story had been expanded on (more lies told). What this was now used for was to add meat to the main charge of attempted murder against Roy Brown. Conspiracy by me, involved with another person, of assaulting Mr Brown and causing him grievous bodily harm, which nearly resulted in his death.

I PLEADED NOT GUILTY

The prosecution opened with a presentation of all the events leading up to my meeting with Mr Brown, and all my insinuations during the divorce proceedings. The prosecution then played several tape recordings of various telephone calls I had made to Mr Brown's home and office. I willingly admitted making these calls, the main ones of which were those made in March after that dreadful visit Lee and I made to try and see his brothers. The night I had drunk too much wine and made a right fool of myself, but I was angry, and it was my only way to hit back. The jury listened as I swore at Carol and Roy Brown. I also made insinuations and said I would take them to court and embarrass them both, especially Brown because he was a divorce solicitor. Within those calls Inspector Dorkins inserted the so-called HITMAN tape recording. So then you heard me talking, and next "Hey Brown, I have the contract on you and I'm going to fucking wrap you up for good."

When I was questioned about that particular call, I stated, as is recorded in the court notes, that I had no idea who it was. But Inspector Dorkins had created an image with the jury, and had already connected me with the HIT MAN recording.

Next day the press and television were full of it:

JEALOUS HUSBAND HIRES HITMAN VIA CONTRACT
THREAT TO MURDER SOLICITOR

They may well have banged the door shut tight then. As far as Mr and Mrs Public were concerned, I WAS GUILTY. They had said so, they had tried and convicted me for the crime. This had happened because Inspector Dorkins had incriminated me by joining the 'Hitman' tape to my recorded phone calls to Brown and Carol - a clear mishandling of evidence.

After the publicity, I suddenly became a celebrity in Walton Jail. On my return from court I would be greeted with MAFIA GODFATHER and other silly jibes many believing I had these dark associations. But if these men did, what were the general public thinking? And more important, the jury who would obviously read the papers or watch television?.

Next came the offers from inmates offering to see Brown off for me. In fact the following letter was shoved under my cell door. When you read it, you will I feel sure realise just how frightening it is being in prison. There are mad people locked up with you, very dangerous men, men with warped ideas on life. This letter frightened me as I'm sure it would have frightened any sane person.

Alright George,

My old friend rumour has it your the man I ought to see. I've heard that your exalent with a "Blade" now I dont know if you smoke but this involves 2oz of burn or a nice piece of cannibis resin, now this is what I want you to do there's a lad on the 5's and he's been giving yours truely fuckin nightmares? Now listen George one of the lads will show you how to assemble a blade with a toothbrush ETC!! and George when this Bastard on the 5s recovers I want to see 3 fuckin Big "MARSBARS" stright down his boatrace!! Well I suppose you want to know who's paying the contract, Well George My old friend I'm of the 1s I've got a short ponytail and you George always wink at me when I'm going PAST the food to be honest George I'm begining to think you fancy Me "alright son"!! Well to be honest with you George I'll be seeing you one of these days Cause Life Sentance's Make Me feel Lonely!! George I'm relieing on you to cut this BASTARD to ribbons Cause I must say you inpressed me with that JOB on MR Brown

Anyway George we'll be in contact again soon!

P.S. George take that ridiculas white coat off man!!

The letter I still have to this day - even the envelope it came in. Can you imagine having to deal with this sort of mind? The writing was neat and clear enough. The setting and spelling I have left as it actually read.

Back in court the prosecution continued its circus, Carol and Mr Brown still sitting there living in their own particular fantasy world. Like actors they repeated their lines to the media, how they were the good guys and I was the nasty old guy. Constantly they can be seen smiling together as the cameras flashed and the fairy story was told. But with every line and every lie they made my chance of freedom impossible.

The police paraded various witnesses which they hoped would add strength to their claim that I was the guilty party. In fact one of the prosecution witnesses was a neighbour of Mr Brown. He swore on oath that he had looked out of his window that morning and actually seen the attacker walking in the close, near Mr Brown's house. He went on to give a description that fitted my own; this included my age, even my grey hair. The Judge told the jury to ignore what he had said, but of course the die was cast. Another neighbour claimed that on the morning in March when Lee and I went to try and see David and Jonathan that I had sat in the car and never got out at all. I had in fact knocked on several doors that morning in an effort to find out where my boys were. This man went on to describe my car as a Volvo saloon. I have never owned or even driven a Volvo saloon!

As poor as this evidence was, it was building a flimsy case and creating an image of me as the guilty man. Even Mrs Grey, Carol's mother made a statement that I had told her I would pay someone to hurt Mr Brown. This statement taken by Inspector Dorkins' colleagues painted a terrible picture of me. Whatever I had said in anger about Carol and Mr Brown had been nothing like what had been concocted. But the jury would hear it and believe it as fact, but it was not. Doris Grey was torn between the truth and her daughter. Carol must have convinced her at some point that I was the attacker. But Doris knew how Carol lied, and she also knew how violent she was. If only Doris Grey had told the police everything then, I don't think I would have come to trial. But the truth was being pushed further and further away from my case.

****

"I know you lawyers can, with ease,
Twist words and meanings as you please;
That language, by your skill made pliant,
Will bend to favour ev'ry client."
John Gay: Fables (1727) *The Dog and the Fox*

CHAPTER EIGHT
A DIRTY FIGHT

ROY Brown was the star player in my first trial and the second for that matter. Hollywood would have been proud of him. There he stood, all 6ft 6inches of him, a young man in his early thirties. A man no stranger to the court room. When the prosecutor attempted to play the contract threat tape, Mr Brown broke down in tears. He held up his hand and said, "Please don't. I don't want to hear it - it frightens me." The learned Judge suggested that Mr Brown sit down to compose himself. Mr Brown then requested a glass of water. This was a very dramatic moment in the trial; he had the jury and he knew it. One of the prison officers with me commented on his performance, saying it was a joke. The trouble was the joke was being played on me and I was not laughing. I'm still not laughing.

Let us go over something here.

Point One: in the Channel 4 'Revenge' programme, January 1995, Mr Brown stated that the attack was a month after the contract threat. The fact is that the call was made in the May, and the attack in the August, three months later.

Once again, five years after the attack. On the television, in view of millions of viewers, Mr Brown broke down in tears as he talked about the attack, still insinuating I was the guilty party as my ex-wife also still does - two years after I have had my sentence quashed!

Point Two: Officer Longfurgoten was never called to either trial. Why was this? Well for a start, he would have had to state that Mr Brown had reported the call to him at Hoylake and stated who he thought the caller was.

Point Three: Mr Brown said he had received only threatening calls from me; he said this in court and perjured himself. Why?

My defence was being buried in lies. I could not believe what was happening to me. Desolate I waited in my cell wondering what on earth I could do now. On one of his visits my barrister Mr Knight asked me if I could remember anything significant that happened prior to me leaving the matrimonial home. I racked my brain, and I poured out all the physical assaults Carol had served out to me. I then told him about the time she went missing in October 1989. The time she went to the Birmingham health club and returned brown as a berry. I relayed the story about her saying she had used the sun beds, and just felt she needed to get away for a few days. Like a fool I had taken it all in.

When Mr Brown next entered the witness box, he swore on oath to tell the truth. He said, and it is fact as recorded by the court, that his affair with my wife, Carol did not commence until January 1990. My barrister then asked Mr Brown a question,

"You have your diary with you. Could you tell me, did you go on holiday in October 1989?"

"Yes," Mr Brown replied.

"Where did you go?" asked my barrister.

"Tenerife."

My barrister then asked a question that floored him.

"Tell me, did Mrs Armstrong arrive?"

Mr Brown's face dropped as he blurted out,

"But that was a coincidence."

But he went on to admit they had met at the airport and had

shared meals together whilst on holiday there. **SOME COINCIDENCE!**

So now we knew for certain they both lied, and they didn't mind doing it in court, even under oath.

Until I heard this in court I had no idea Carol had been in Tenerife with Brown. You will recall I had given her passport to the police after reporting her missing. She had 'nipped to the shops' you will recall, leaving her children without a word. So how had she obtained another passport? And why did she need other passports ?. You well may ask.

The trial went on with Mr Brown continuing to give a first rate performance at every opportunity. But the fact was that he was having an affair with a client, and he had lied under oath - a solicitor, a man trusted to uphold the law. So it should have been clear to all that he had acted in a most unprofessional way and didn't mind bending the truth when he felt justified. To remind you, our decree nisi was not declared until August 24th 1990, and until Carol left our home in December 1989 we were still living as a family for the sake of the boys.

You will also recall that I had instigated the divorce in 1986 after suffering her violent outbursts long enough and being aware she was not entirely faithful.

But a strange thing had started to occur whilst the divorce was going through. Carol would instigate rows and then tape record them. I was not aware of this at the time, but was to find out later. I am convinced now this was all part and parcel of a ploy to make me look the villain of the piece.

You must remember that there was a time when Carol would have been entitled to a very large settlement of money from the insurance from the Pavilion fire. I had agreed on a large settlement for the sake of the children. Fate was to cheat us both of that money.

In the box, Mr Brown continued reporting the numerous phone

calls from me; many he said he had not recorded. More lies. Thankfully his conduct was not only scorned by me, the legal profession in general were not enamoured with the actions of Mr Brown. I have a document in my possession that clearly states that it is common knowledge that the many in the legal fraternity feel that Mr Brown has brought the profession into disrepute by his behaviour, compounding the said mistake by giving interviews and posing for photographs for the press. I wonder how they feel now he has appeared on television!

For now, the first trial continued, Mr Brown never leaving a dry eye in the place. I can see him now, his handkerchief in his hand as he wept, then the shaky hand to sip a drop of water.

Next to come along was poor Doris Grey. She now had to relate conversations I had had with her. She told how I threatened to take Mr Brown through every court in the land, how I would disgrace him. The remarks I had made, remarks any husband would make to his mother-in-law when he finds his wife carrying on and leaving the children. But now the facts were all distorted. The police had convinced her I was guilty of attempted murder. Doris was confused and upset. At first she refused to go to court, but Inspector Dorkins threatened to arrest her if she didn't. On the first day of the trial they had to almost drag her out to make an appearance.

Doris was afraid; she did not want to have to lie, and she did not want to have her words twisted. She knew there was more to this; she knew Carol better than most. Doris told me afterwards that at the time Carol and Roy had started visiting her, bringing her presents, but prior to that time they had practically ignored her. Now Carol and Roy played a different tune and they used her as another instrument in their great orchestration of lies.

The press, the television, the nation were told I was a Mafia Godfather. Grandfather yes. But Godfather! If it had not been so damning, it was laughable. On my return to the prison from court the prisoners made more jibes, many convinced I was involved with the Mafia. Others who knew I was a good guy really joked with me, but none of it was funny I can assure you.

When I was placed on bail, I actually had someone offer me the service of a hit man to do Brown properly. Yes I mean it. I turned away from any such offer, but the thought still chills me. Mr Brown though amazes me, particularly his going on television recently. The real culprit is still out there as I was always innocent, and they both must know that. Still they are willing to court with fate. What is more worrying for me is the safety of little Jonathan and David, the two sons Lee and I have still not seen in all these passing years. There is something very cruel in that and brings into question their kindness.

Doris Grey did her bit under duress, but oddly she was never played the contract threat tape! I wonder why. Don't you think that was very odd? Well the truth is she would have recognised the voice, as she did later when the tape recording was played to her. They didn't want Doris to blow the case out of the window. But if that hypothosis is true, it implies that they knew it wasn't me! Well I'm sure all three of them knew it wasn't me, but it did not suit their purpose to let anyone else know that.

The contract threat tape was used to cover a gaping whole in the prosecution case. There was no case, but I fitted the bill and the Bill helped fit me up.

Some months after my imprisonment, which as things were going was inevitable, my friends Mr and Mrs Smith would go over to the Wirral and visit Doris Grey. At that meeting they played her a copy of the recording. This was eighteen months after I was convicted. The police had refused to let me have a copy until then. I had however persisted in my request and they eventually relented. With that in hand I could start my own investigation.

As soon as Mrs Grey heard the tape, she said, "That's Terry Lyed." She has since made a statement to that effect. She also stated that whilst the tape was played in court, she was kept in the witness area well out of ear shot.

But again that was a distant world away from the here and now. In court that day Doris Grey looked strained in the witness box, and she broke down. It was brought out that she had her own misfortune and that she had experienced problems with drinking and an unfortunate previous marriage. This information obviously made her look a weak witness for either side. Mr Brown actually highlighted her unfortunate predicament by as good as saying she was a drunk or mentally ill.

Yes, no stone was left unturned by 'The Lovers' as they were called by Channel 4. If they have so much love, they have shown little to those who have encountered their world.

When Doris Grey left the box, I stood up and said loudly that she should not have had to go through that.

Next came star witness Number Two, my Carol. She looked demure, and she is a beautiful woman, I cannot deny that.

She was asked various questions about me, then asked why she went to Tenerife in 1989.

"Just to get away from it all," she replied.

Here now was a chance for my counsel to strip her lie for lie. How she went out saying she was just going shopping, the passport, the financial aspect with regard to travel arrangements. Booking the hotel, the meals with Roy Brown. The questioning continued, but my counsel was failing to draw attention to these vital points. If he had, the prosecution would have tumbled like a pack of cards.

She then went on as she was questioned to admit she had loved the quality of lifestyle which I had provided for her for over ten years. The holidays, all over the world. The luxury homes, the expensive cars. There was no mention of her false driving licences. In fact when she did pass, a year after her first try, she took great delight by phoning me and saying,

"Not bad eh, all those years and you did not even know. Ha, ha,". Funny to her maybe, but that meant she had been driving around putting our children at risk.

But the star was still being questioned, and the next reply shocked me beyond measure. She was asked if she had liked the lifestyle. She replied yes, but I had no freedom. My counsel said "No Freedom? But you had children and a beautiful home, holidays, clothing galore, everything most young ladies want."

The star replied, "Yes, but I wanted freedom. I even discussed it with my friend Janis who said, 'Hang on, he has not long to go." I said, You are kidding.' "

"Why?" asked my counsel.

"You are joking. His mother lived till she was eighty odd and his Dad is still alive," she finished.

Again my counsel didn't profit by this obvious line of thought. She wished me dead, and she would do anything to get me out of the way, and so seeing me tucked up in prison was no hardship for her.

In this climate of ill feeling for me I feel my counsel could have flushed out how she had become violent and had caused injury to me. But no, she was left to guard that secret.

When asked a question about Terry Lyed who, I might add, became very close to her, her reply was that he, Lyed, would do anything for money. Then she admitted she and Roy Brown went along and reported the call in May 1990.

The jury never was told that Terry Lyed had visited Roy Brown's home on two occasions prior to the attack. On the first visit he was threatening and abusive; his wife was with him at the time and she was screaming and shouting as per Roy Brown's statement. So it was obvious there was at least one other person with a grievance against Brown. Who can say how many others may have wanted to injure him?

On went the trial, and I had to sit there taking blow for blow. I watched as my freedom slipped away from me. If this had been a fight, I would have felt my seconds had thrown in the towel on me.

Yes, I am bitter about that, as I never should have been con-

117

victed. I sometimes wonder whose side my counsel was on. I was very green. Maybe I didn't understand the law. Whatever it was, I felt powerless to help myself at all and I was losing faith in those who were supposed to be on my side.

Carol nearly got her wish, for I nearly died in prison, but my children are worth fighting for. So is the truth.

So where and how did Terry Lyed come by Mr Brown's home address and phone number? Why did he have them? My counsel didn't bother to ask.

Now let me tell you this. On the morning Mr Brown was attacked, the attacker said, "Mr Brown, I'm James". The name happened to be the same name as Carol's first husband. It also just happens Terry Lyed and James Tilbery have been bosom pals since school days. Coincidence? Does it mean anything? One thing is sure - the police ignored all that and went all out for me. A man of sixty-one, a grandfather of eleven. Not a Mafia Godfather. When they sentenced me, they sentenced my whole family. I can't forgive them for that.

When the star had concluded her appearance in the witness box, she was followed by Inspector Dorkins. When asked to consider doing a voice comparison regarding the hit man contract tape, he replied, "Not necessary - we had the right man."

It seems hard to credit that he said that, but he did. I wonder if he really believed it? I doubt it, or was he that stupid? Whatever the case, he mishandled the evidence. He linked my telephone calls to Carol and Roy on that March night to the contract threat. He made an edit joining them all together. This implied to the jury that I had made all the calls. This was a most unethical move on his part, and I'm amazed it was even allowed. But it was, and it was that tape that did it.

When Roy Brown was in hospital, it was Inspector Dorkins who met Carol at Manchester airport. You will recall she was supposed to be in London on a modelling assignment. She was in fact at a

Hotel with another man, something again I was to learn much, much later.

The Inspector picked her up, then took her to the hospital. Whilst Roy was in hospital, Inspector Dorkins continued to visit Carol questioning her with regard to her own whereabouts the night before the attack. Whatever he learnt he must have kept to himself. One thing is clear - over the next eight months before I was to come to trial, suffering the misery of prison for a crime I didn't commit, Inspector Dorkins became a close friend of Carol and Mr Brown. On one occasion in the second trial, Carol walked into the court, quickly went up to the Inspector, reached for his hand and then proceeded to kiss him on the side of the face. Another morning she arrived with him in his car. This was witnessed by three other people who knew her.

But let us return to the farce of the first trial. Like some entertaining floor show, the prosecution put up large speakers in the court room and played the contract threat tape.

"Who is it?" they quizzed me.

"I haven't a clue," I answered.

"We think that is the man you hired," they pointed out.

"It's ridiculous. I haven't a clue who it is," I again replied.

But I was all washed up. The months of press coverage that Carol and Roy had engaged in had condemned me. The world had been painted a vision of a hard man, a cruel man who had beaten up his wife. CHAMPAGNE CHARLIE MADE MY LIFE HELL was one headline, this one being printed before Roy Brown was even attacked. They were brilliant at self-publicity. They had me hung drawn and quartered. I had arrived in court a broken man, but I was to be broken further. It would have suited them both well if I had died, but I'm still here. They have had me eating canvas long enough. Their last publicity venture is about to back fire. They have gone on television and lied in glorious technicolour.

The day soon arrived when it was my turn to enter the witness box. I was terrified, but felt sure my innocence would shine through and that thought kept me strong. It's all I had left.

My barrister, Mr White, commenced questioning me and to prove my innocence to the jury. His approach was dramatic in emphasis and he managed to draw attention to various issues I have pointed out to you. For my part I was naïve and blind to my own vulnerability.

Several times I tried to speak up for myself, correcting certain points, but I was told by Mr White, in a subtle and very kind way, to keep quiet. I confess this is not an easy thing for me, as I do like to put my point over. Here I felt gagged and tied; there were so many things I wanted to tell the court, and I was frustrated by the fact there were vital points that should have been brought to light. Looking back, and I do with bitterness about the whole thing, I now realize, that if I had been able to make clear my points and give the jury the information that was available, I would have been found NOT GUILTY. I would have saved the taxpayers in excess of ONE MILLION POUNDS. I would have saved all the heartache my family have been put through.

Next I was handed over to the prosecution. Now it was Mr Black's turn. At this time I was not aware Mr Black and Mr White were in fact colleagues. Their offices were in the same chambers. Whilst I appreciate this is not an unusual occurrence, I am convinced the old school tie network was at work here. I will recount another incident that took place in London at my appeal that points to this. But we are a long way from there yet.

The prosecution questioned me for several hours. I was exhausted. Ten days I was ferried to court, then back to prison. Throughout this time, the press, the radio and television continued to paint me as a sinister figure, HIRED A HIT MAN. What chance had I got? I had already been tried by the media and found guilty! It would have been impossible for the jury to think me NOT GUILTY. Every day, in black and white and verbally they were told otherwise.

When the prosecution had finished questioning me, his Honour Justice Crowe began summing up, which took some time, and I have to say he was fair to me in every way. Then the time came for the jury to retire.

I felt faint at this point, and my head was spinning. There was a numbness about my whole being. There had been a time when I thought things would never have gone this far, that I would have been released months ago. Now all these months later, I knew only too well how REAL this all was.

There were people locked in a room talking about me! They were about to judge me! If anyone had told me this was going to happen to me, I would have laughed in their face. I would have asked how that could possibly happen to an innocent man. Well I was in for a rude awakening. It had happened, and I was that innocent man.

So once again I was marched down to the cells beneath the court. I was placed in amongst other prisoners who were also from Walton Jail. These men were also appearing in court to face charges for various crimes they were suspected of committing. Unlike me however they had not gained unwelcome notoriety and condemnation. They still had a chance for justice.

Several hours passed, and then I heard my name called out. One inmate said, "This is it George. Good luck!" Others nodded and wished me well. I was terrified, a feeling I was learning to live with. The ritual began; as always I was handcuffed. I was then taken to the lift and up we went into the court. It had been like that each day, but now the fear trembled in me.

The court was crowded. My relatives and friends were all there to give me moral support. I looked over at Mr and Mrs Smith who had so kindly looked after my son Lee these past eight months. I then looked at at Lee's mother who had ignored him throughout that time. My eyes looked over to my sons by my previous marriage of

36 years. They had stood by me all this time, as had their mother my first wife Lilian. I bowed my head in hidden shame and inner tears. How could I have ever been so foolish? I had thrown away all that was good for a woman who now watched this charade with her solicitor boyfriend.

I tried to stand tall, I tried to put on a brave face for the sake of those who genuinely cared, but I was a broken man. Eight long months in Walton Jail had changed me.

All eyes were on me as I walked into that court room. Fixed and cold were the looks from Carol and Roy Brown as they sat there hand in hand awaiting my sentence with baited breath. The silence was deathly as the jury returned. Next the clerk was asked to give the verdict.

The foreman stood up and said, "We are unable to come to a decision." My heart was thumping. I was shocked. The court rustled and suddenly the chatter grew like a wave until it became louder. Several press men left, hot footed to make their calls about the MAFIA GODFATHER no doubt. The judge spoke and order prevailed. He instructed the jury as to the recognised procedure and the jury retired again.

Down again I was taken to the cells. This time the prisoners seemed to think it was a good sign that the jury had not agreed. To me, it was all crazy. How could they honestly believe I had done this, or arranged it? Two or three hours now passed; time had never been so slow. Eventually the two officers came to collect me. Surely this time I was going up in the lift for the last time. Soon I would hear NOT GUILTY and be a free man. I would be able to go home with my son Lee.

I stood there in the accused box and moments seemed like hours. The foreman stood and informed the Judge that the jury could not agree. The court rippled again with quiet chatter.

The Judge once again spoke to the jurors and once again they had to retire. Down I went again, down to the familiar cells, down to those dark depths of terror. Would I ever be free again? The prisoners who were still down there felt sure I was as good as free.

"George, you are free if they return again," they told me. I wished I could have felt so positive about things. But I had lost all faith in the truth and justice. I was convinced I had been set up. God knows why, but someone certainly had a lot to hide.

When I came up for the last time, I was literally shaking in the box.

The words of the foreman rang out. NO DECISION.

My relatives shouted with elation, whilst I just stood there. I couldn't understand what was going on. The Judge then quietened everyone as the press hot footed away to the nearest telephone in a bid to be first with the story.

My barrister Mr White, then came over to me to explain what would happen next. He told me there would be a new trial. The Prosecutor was insisting on it. Later I was told that on certain occasions if a no decision is met, the case can be dismissed. In this case however that was not to be the way of it.

The Honourable Judge began to explain the procedure, during which time he spoke across the court room to my counsel. He said "There was something you wanted Mr White?"

I am now convinced that Judge Crowe thought I was innocent. This was his way of telling my counsel to apply for bail - which he did almost immediately. My head swam. Was I free? What could he mean by a new trial? Not for me surely? Perhaps they meant for the real attacker. My mind just would not take all of this in. It seemed the bad dream was not quite over.

****

The 1960s and 70s

Top left: Gold Cup winner
Mecca, 1962. I beat 97
other managers.

Top right: Ken Dodd, master
of mirth, putting sunshine
into some of the staff at
the Plaza, Birkenhead.

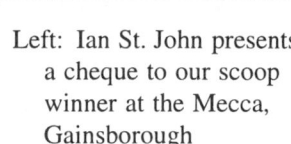

Left: Ian St. John presents
a cheque to our scoop
winner at the Mecca,
Gainsborough

Above: Standing by the
cut-out photo of the
Hillman Imp car I would
later be presented with.

CHAPTER NINE
COURT OF CONTEMPT

I WAS allowed on bail until a new trial date could be fixed. It was planned that I would reside with my son Gary in Southport. He had offered to do this and I was very grateful as my own house had now been sold. Gary stored what little I had together with my clothing.

Back down in the cells the prisoners greeted me with great excitement. They patted me on the back and shook my hand. I was overwhelmed by it all, my tears and laughter mingling unsure of my emotions.

At the time, because this was all knew to me, I did not make much of the fact my counsel had not taken the time to come down and congratulate me. But later I came to realise that I would have questionable support with all things legal.

When bail had been processed, I was taken to the reception area to be greeted by friends and relations. Several of them broke down and cried with me. As we left press and photographers, my old pal Carl Eaden endeavoured to shield me to stop them from getting to me. Also present was Allan Williams, another good old pal. From there my sons, and friends which included Mr and Mrs Smith went along to the Holiday Inn. On the way there in Mark's car, my younger son by my first marriage, Mark, broke down, and I did too. Here was the baby of the first Armstrong family. He was 22 years old, a young man now. After all these lies he still believed in me, he still loved me. That affection warmed my chilled heart. I love Mark dearly as I love all my children, it's so tragic that sometimes it takes a tragedy to let those feelings really come to the surface.

At the Holiday Inn I rang Lee at Mr and Mrs Smiths' house and explained I would have to stay at Gary's house that night but would pick him up first thing next morning. Lee was over the moon.

I had deliberately asked Mr and Mrs Smith to keep Lee away from the courts. I didn't want him seeing me in the state I was in. Nor did I want him watching his mother and her boyfriend sitting there watching me. He was far too young to cope with any of this.

When I had made my phone calls, I rejoined the group who by now had purchased six bottles of champagne. My pal Carl Eaden pushed money into my hand and the whole time spent there was wonderful. I had arranged to pop in and visit Lil on the way to Southport, which we eventually did. But there was much to talk about. For instance, when I was arrested, Carl Eaden and some other friends of mine had also been arrested. For the benefit of Mr Brown, they were then placed on an identity parade instigated by Inspector Dorkins. But the plan turned into another farce when Mr Brown picked out none of them. Instead he chose a man who happened to be a solicitor's clerk.

We may have laughed about that, but we were laughing at anything. I felt so happy to be amongst people I knew and loved.

When the welcome back home party was over, Mark drove me over to see his mother Lil. From there I went along to Gary's house in Southport. Next day Gary arranged a hire car which was a tremendous help for me whilst on bail. My first port of call was to go along to the Prince of Wales. I sat in there and took coffee whilst I planned my arrangements regarding my son Lee. I had spoken to him that morning and was to pick him up from school at 4 p.m. Gary had agreed to let Lee stay with me at his home until I could make alternative arrangements which I did eventually, thank God.

Sadly whilst I stayed with Gary, several national newspapers had found out where I was living, and poor Gary had the embarrassment to contend with. Once again the headlines read:

GEORGE ARMSTRONG, THE JEALOUS HUSBAND WHO HAD HIRED A CONTRACT HIT MAN TO MURDER A SOLICITOR.

Several people tried to contact me after this. One person who did make contact turned out to be very important. Her name was Mrs Kemp whom I met in a rather odd way.

One day I drove Lee to Southport train station to pop in and buy a newspaper at the kiosk there. Whilst there, Lee spotted his mother just getting out of her car. I stopped and allowed Lee to run over and see her. He was excited, as he had not seen her for a quite a while now. It was clear he wanted to go over to her. I allowed him to do so. They chatted and she told him what her arrangements were. She was celebrating her birthday at the Café Bar, and she suggested that Lee and I should call in there later in the afternoon. Lee was over the moon. Suddenly he now had his Dad and his Mum close by, and he was ecstatic. For Lee's sake I drove back to the Café Bar at 2.30 and let Lee go in to see his Mum. About twenty minutes later Lee appeared with his mother, and they came across to the car. I noticed Carol was holding a glass of champagne which she held out and said it was for me. I refused it, and so Carol drank it herself. We talked a little and Carol several times asked me to go into the Café Bar with her and take some refreshment. I shook my head to say no.

I was only there for Lee, she is after all his mother. Throughout her requests for me to join her, she said,

"Don't worry, he's not there."

I replied, "I couldn't care less."

She persisted but I refused to leave the car. She also repeated several times.

"You know George, I've got one now I can't get shut of. He's a pain. Guess who."

Carol looked lovely as usual, she always had done. In the past I had doted on her. In those early days she had everything money could buy - she also had my love. But when the money ran out, Carol changed. After the disastrous fire at the Pavilion, our world was to begin to crumble. There would be no going back and suddenly I had become of no use to her. But God only knows why she was a party to the suffering I have experienced via two trials and a prison sentence that could have killed me off.

I looked at her now she spoke of Roy Brown coldly like this. Frankly, he was welcome to her. As she continued, a lady came out of the Café Bar and came over to the car. She introduced herself as Mrs Kemp, a friend of Carol's. Carol and Lee wondered off back to the Café Bar and Mrs Kemp went to follow. As she did so, she asked where we were staying, saying quickly, "Can I ring you?".

I said yes, and gave her my son's phone number. Soon after Lee returned to the car and we continued our day together.

When I arrived home that evening, I was given a phone number. Mrs Kemp had rung me and left her number. I rang her back and arranged to meet her in Southport at midday the following day. She implied that there were several things she wanted to talk to me about but she wouldn't say any more over the phone.

Next day Lee and I drove into Southport and met Mrs Kemp. After coffee and general conversation she disclosed certain information that amazed me. In the first instance she told me she had been friendly with Carol for some considerable time. They had socialized quite a lot together, but now Mrs Kemp was shocked by Carol's behaviour. It transpired that a close male friend of Mrs Kemp had become attracted to Carol, and that she had uncovered some unsavoury news. Mrs Kemp, it turned out, had introduced Carol to a gentleman when they were attending Haydock races. Mrs Kemp told me they had frequented Haydock races together on various occasions, but on this particular day Carol had courted the deliberate attention of this particular gentleman and he had become attracted to her.

Mrs Kemp then went on to tell me that the man was from London. Further she told me this was the gentleman she was with the night Roy Brown was attacked. Carol it seems had been with the gentleman for two days.

I was staggered. What was this all about? You will recall when Carol flew back from London, and the so alleged modelling assignment. She was taken to see Roy Brown in hospital where they had a tearful reunion. After that, Inspector Dorkins had driven Carol home. But why, oh why didn't this come to light? The police must have known about her true whereabouts. We know for a fact Carol was questioned by the police as to her whereabouts and her possible duplicity. Still she came out of there smelling of roses. It just doesn't make sense.

From my side I am still disgusted with her total disregard for Jonathan and David throughout this time.

Where had she left them? And who with? Mrs Kemp told me she had looked after the boys many times. She and many others by the sound of it.

Mrs Kemp told me Carol was actually at the opening of a restaurant in London the night before the attack. So it was patently clear that probably all the so-called modelling assignments were a ruse for going off and enjoying herself.

But why lie? Roy Brown knew Carol met other men. Maybe she knew he had other lovers too? A strange relationship, a modern one maybe, but what it points to is the fact there were people out there who possibly really DID HAVE A JEALOUSY PROBLEM. Somehow these were conveniently swept under the carpet. They were PROTECTED.

It was easier to pin the blame on me. What worries me more than anything is this. My two sons could have been there in that house with Roy Brown that morning he was attacked. The mad man who attacked Roy Brown could have murdered my children. A man who is still out there, enjoying freedom and no blame.

Ask yourself this. Who knew Roy Brown was in the house on his own? For a start Carol knew. Roy Brown knew.

Mrs Kemp went on to disclose that when Inspector Dorkins had dropped Carol back home from the hospital, Carol rang Mrs Kemp and asked her to come over to the house and clear up the mess that had been created by this attack. Mrs Kemp agreed and left her interests in Southport and went across to assist Carol.

Whilst she helped Carol with the cleaning up, Carol told Mrs Kemp who she had been with that night and why. Mrs Kemp said she was disgusted.

With this new information at hand I asked if she would talk to my legal representative and give him this new evidence. I now hoped that with more proof of lies and deceit the truth could and would come out.

Armed with this fresh evidence I felt encouraged to look to the future. The next trial would bring the truth off the ropes, and the lies they were telling would eventually tie them in knots. So for now I could concentrate on Lee, and try and build towards better times for us both.

Nothing came easy. I was still having to fight all the way for every little grasp of sanity and justice. The court would later give me permission to lease a house in Magull and allow my son Lee to live with me there. In this way his schooling would have some continuity. On the business front I resumed trying to open my business in Kirkby. I had already spent approximately £200,000 in transforming The Cherryfield Social Club and it was vital I moved on with this project for mine and Lee's future security. But being on bail, I was to find progress very difficult.

It was now that I had a call from my nephew Gordon Twist. I had not seen him for sixteen years; he was the son of my sister Gwen whom I also had not seen for a number of years. What a pity they didn't stay out of my life completely! My sister and her boy came into my life when I was at an all time low. They proceeded to ensure that I was pushed even lower down the ladder of heartache and misery. But let me tell you the story, and pray your relatives don't serve you like this.

Gordon and I had a nice chat on the phone and I arranged to meet him in the Prince of Wales Hotel in Southport. During our discussion I informed him of my efforts with regard to The Cherry-field Social Club. From there, I took him along and showed him the premises. He was amazed. I introduced him to the Manageress, who seemed very impressed with him. He gave the impression he was financially sound and knew what he was about. Later this would prove to be untrue. He was neither.

With the trial over my head, and my problems with bail dissipating my efforts to go into business. Gordon Twist appeared to be the ideal man to hold the fort for me until all my legal commitments had been resolved. It seemed at the time the only answer. He was after all family, my sister's son. I could trust him surely. So I signed over everything to him. I entrusted him with all that I had. It was understood that he would then become a fifty-fifty partner on my return to a business standing. That day would never dawn I'm afraid. My sister and my nephew robbed Lee and me of any possible chance of making good with the Cherryfield.

When my sentence was quashed and I became free, they refused to let me be a part of the business. My sister even said I had threatened her son in an attempt to regain what was mine. I suppose she thought she may as well jump on the bandwagon. After all I was a safe bet; I had been convicted once. But how can your own sister do this? As it turned out, they would eventually bankrupt the Cherryfield. In doing so they cheated Lee and me out of any chance of a future in that business. But then if I had not been in this terrible position I would never have had to trust in others. Because of this ridiculous case I would lose everthing.

The new trial was now on the horizon, and was set for June 1991. The months had passed so quickly that now I started to dread the spectre of another trial. Surely this time the case would be thrown out. Besides I had more evidence - I was a little wiser now.

Throughout the time I was on bail, Lee and I had had some wonderful times together. Somehow all the bad things were swept away when we two buddies were on form. We both missed Jonathan and David. I still cannot understand why they kept Lee apart from his brothers. I think this was very cruel of them both.

On June 13th 1991 my second trial began. The jury were sworn in and the second travesty was set in motion. The procedures were all very much the same as the first trial. There were the legal discussions and then we went through another performance by Roy Brown, followed by witnesses. But one witness who should have been there, a witness not even called in my first trial, was once again strangely absent. The man was the officer who took Roy Brown's statement the night he received the contract threat call. The missing witness was Officer Longfurgoten. You will recall it was this officer who attended to Roy Brown, when he and Carol went along to Hoylake police station on May 25th 1990, the day after the call. The non-appearance of this witness clearly points to the fact that Inspector Dorkins did not want the jury to know that Roy Brown had thought someone else wanted to harm him. The silence of Roy Brown and Inspector Dorkins in this matter was clearly a conspiracy to place all blame overtly upon me.

If Officer Longfurgoten had been called on the first trial, the facts would have been there for the court to evaluate. Instead it became evidence withheld. On this basis how could I have a fair trial?

Surely my counsel could have done something about this? But then I have to ask myself if they were a party to all this? Was it THE LAW versus GEORGE ARMSTRONG? It certainly felt like it. But there was more drama to come. With the new information I had been given from Mrs Kemp, I felt confident that I could shed light on the devious and promiscuous lifestyle Carol had indulged in.

I had to subpoena Mrs Kemp to appear. Whilst she had at first agreed to speak up for me, for some reason she had not been over willing to come forward. It was however vital she came to tell the jury what she had told me. Surely when they were told about the other men in Carol's life, they could see how very likely it was that any number of close acquaintances could be the possible culprit. The same could be said for Roy Brown and his social life.

Maybe he had upset someone in business? Or could it be one of Carol's suitors? Maybe it was Carol. She had after all told me "I'VE GOT ONE I CAN'T GET SHUT OF NOW."

This, from one half of the pair they called THE LOVERS on a television programme. What a joke!

On day two, Mrs Kemp arrived with two police escorts. I looked over to her - she seemed tense. I was puzzled as to why she had the police with her. On the first day she had arrived on her own, sat there and quietly listened. I could understand her nervousness. A court room is a frightening place. But then I was given the opportunity to speak to her. Her words were guarded, she looked upset, when she told me she couldn't give evidence. I looked at her, I felt my face stiffen, my tongue scramble to ask why. She then went on to say that the night before she had received a phone call. She was threatened that if she gave evidence on my behalf she would be sorry. She had been told she would have to leave her Southport business and get of town. This is why she had been escorted by police to the court room. She had reported the calls to them and they were there to make sure she arrived safely. Unfortunately these calls continued for the rest of that week. Mrs Kemp did not turn up at the court again until the last day of the trial.

I was devastated by this news. What the hell was happening? Why weren't the police looking into this further? Why hadn't they set up a tape recorder to hear these threats? Why wasn't my legal representative exploiting this new turn of events? It was vital this threat was brought to light. But, no, that was not to be. In fact Mrs Kemp told me that her private phone number was ex-directory, only a few close friends and relatives knew it. Two people who certainly did know it were Carol and Roy Brown.

Whatever this was all about I cannot say. What I can report is that in view of this, the Judge would not let Mrs Kemp give evidence. It sounds crazy - it was crazy. Another morsel of evidence that could have made a meal of that silly trial. But no, still the lies and shadows shook hands with one another.

As the days went on, I tried to keep faith in what little justice was left for me. They say faith can move mountains, but all I wanted it to do was stand by the truth. After all the truth so far had been trampled on by some heavyweight liars. But now it was my turn to receive a call, and I had rigged up a recording device in case I should be a victim of a threatening call myself. But when I heard the voice I was shocked. It was Carol on the other end of the line. At first she just chatted, general conversation.

Then she said "Roy said you should have taken that offer, as now you will go to prison for five to ten years."

This referred to a situation that had occurred during the earlier part of that day. What I mean by that is, the prosecution offered me a deal. The deal was this: if I pleaded guilty to threatening to kill Brown on the Sunday morning visit in March, when I took Lee to try and see his brothers, then they would drop the conspiracy charge.

Once I had capitulated on this, then I would be able to go home with just a charge of assault. I couldn't believe the audacity of the prosecution with regard to this suggestion. Naturally I refused their offer. What in fact they were asking me to do was lie! I had made no such threat on that Sunday morning or at any other time. On the telephone that evening when I made my calls to him and Carol, I told him I would finish him as a solicitor. The only threat of violence from me was a rather foolish gesture. I had once told Roy Brown I would get my brother to punch him on the nose. In view of the way he had been party to keeping my children from me, I would have thought that was a quite normal attempt to get back at him. It was an act of sheer frustration.

But to get back to Carol ringing me. Don't you think that was a most obnoxious act? She had literally put the knife in and sought to turn it. After her call, I rang my barrister who said "Bring that tape in." So next day I did so, and Mr White listened to it. He then called over the prosecution and played it to him. When he had played it again I was asked to leave. Within a short time Carol was called in by them for questioning. Incredibly Carol denied she had made any such call. She even accused me of making it up. Not satisfied with this response, it was decided the tape should be analysed by the police. So it was sent to the police headquarters at Preston; this tape was thought to be so important it was carried by a dispatch rider.

Now to back pedal a little. Don't you think it's odd that so much trouble was taken to voice check this tape? You will recall that when Inspector Dorkins was asked about obtaining a voice check with my voice and that of the contract tape, he said "There's no need. We have the right man." I'm afraid it's painfully clear there was a *conspiracy* to nail me for a crime I did not commit. God knows why and so do a handful of others.

So the voice check was made using the recorded call she insisted she had not made. The reply came back, it was official. The experts had made their comparisons and the answer was printed in black and white on crisp snow white paper.

The voice was hers - she had made the call. Carol had no alternative but to confess. Yes, it was her. Yes she had made that call. So the liar had been snared in her own cruel attempt to cause me more anguish. So now both barristers knew she lied, but they knew this wasn't the first time. It was uncovered that she had lied about her whereabouts the night before the attack on Roy Brown. She had maintained the fictitious modelling assignment story which Inspector Dorkins had obviously swallowed hook line and sinker.

Later however she had to be questioned again by the police for over three hours. It was apparent that at that time they thought

Carol might have been trying to *kill two birds with one stone.* Losing both Roy and me. Carol was also not too slow in putting others in the frame either. Terry Lyed, her sister's husband, was offered for bait. She told the police "He would do anything for money."

Carol's lying was now becoming legendary. For some odd reason she had earlier told the police her mother had died of cancer! A file note from the case purports - Carol is a congenital liar and lies just for the sake of it without gaining any advantage by doing so on occasions.

The prosecution had no alternative but to dismiss with her services as a witness. To put it bluntly, they threw her out because she continually lied. In view of this, WHY was I there? She and Roy Brown had lied. Their lies had placed me in prison for eight months. I was now going through a second trial for *Attempted Murder.* It's incredible that they got away with doing this to me. They assassinated my character and ruined my life. If I had died in prison, they would have got away with murder.

I don't say this lightly. It is a fact Roy Brown was party to the deceit about Carol's mother supposedly being dead. It is also a fact *he lied in court.* He denied a relationship with Carol, only to be proved a liar by them holidaying together.

In court he maintained their relationship started in January 1990, when in fact they were both in Tenerife in 1989. To compound this, Carol had used one of several passports she had acquired. When questioned about which passport she used for this liaison, Roy Brown said "Carol Armstrong must have deceived me." How right he was. But deception seemed to come easy to both of them. Brown had stated he finished with a lady he had been going strong with in October 1989, a lady who would be devastated when Carol came on the scene. A lady who perhaps would be enraged to find out Carol and Roy had had an illicit few days together in Tenerife.

In truth there were many avenues of investigation that could have been taken by the police; there were other suspects. But since all had been overlooked or ignored, none of this was helping me. In the first trial I spoke up and interrupted, constantly being told to keep quiet. In this trial I had been told I must not speak up. I was told it would not help my case at all. I was wrong to listen to that advice.

By now I was seen by the world as this monster. A jealous husband, a man with *Underworld Connections*, a night club owner. I ran *Bingo Halls* for God's sake. A place for Moms and Dads. My venture into the night club world was ancillary and all above board. But the mud had been continually thrown. The newspapers were particularly guilty in this respect. I was the MAFIA GODFATHER who had arranged A HIT MAN. What chance did I have?

It seemed all the stops were out now, and Roy Brown went for gold when he again went into the witness box. Whilst giving evidence he broke down and cried, "Don't play the contract threat tape, it frightens me." The Judge even gave him a cup of water whilst he sat down. I looked on. I kept silent as instructed. I felt defeated. I wish I had spoken up; things couldn't have been any worse. Or could they? Unfortunately yes.

The prosecution pulled out a Merseyside Police interview record dated the 14th of May 1989. This was a supposed attack I had made on Mike Whitewash, the night I had been invited to his home. This being Carol's cousin - Carol was also present at the time. If you can remember back, I had spent most of the day with Mike Whitewash who was arranging for me to meet Carol to talk over things. Mike was drunk when I arrived and after staggering about at the door, an argument ensued. On reflection I do feel this was all a bit stage-managed. Now however it was being used as more evidence of my so-called aggressive behaviour. I must remind you I was interviewed about this so-called attack ten days after that date. I think that was very odd. I can't help feeling he was possibly pushed into reporting this supposed attack. Either way, nothing had happened, possibly to the disappointment of someone whom I shall not name. I leave that for you to ponder over.

From my point of view this was just another black mark against me as far as the jury was concerned.

Then came Mr Brown's last minute witness, Violet Mist, or should I call her 'Lost in a Mist'? Violet Mist claimed she was present the day I visited Mr Brown's office. Violet Mist, had been an articled clerk to Mr Brown at that time. In her statement, and I have the actual copy, she said she was working in the same office as Roy Brown, when I called on him in September 1988. This was the day I went to see what he looked like. If you recall, in the June I had been conveniently left a letter regarding the forthcoming birth of David. Since this time his calls to Carol had become more frequent and I wanted to see what he was all about.

A portion of the letter I will now quote. The letter is dated the 3rd of June 1988.

By the time you receive this letter you may well in fact have produced Jonathan or worse still from my point of view, be about to produce him! Whatever your circumstances may be, can you please telephone me when convenient to call in and swear the affidavit so that the matter can proceed.

This is the letter Carol had claimed featured a kiss in the signature. This letter is on professional headed note paper. Tell me, does that read like a solicitor-client relationship? I think not. Yet they still maintained their affair had not started until January 1990. Who are they kidding?

So yes, I went along to his office, A stupid move I grant you, but I've paid hard for my stupidity. So Violet Mist had been there and heard me threaten Roy Brown. The statement by the way was not made until February 14th 1991. Was it some coincidence that this was made on *Valentine's Day*? Should we read anything in that? I don't really know. One thing is clear - her memory of what took place is vivid. More than two years had passed by but nothing had dulled her account. She also said she had been at the court when the injunction was enforced, and again gave value to her statement by saying Carol was afraid of me. This was very useful, and it is such a pity he makes no mention of her in his statement regarding that meeting.

The mysterious Violet Mist had been offered as a witness in the first trial at the last moment. My counsel made the comment - was she giving a true account? Or had she discussed the matter with Mr Brown? Connived with him to give an account which wholly exaggerated what really happened? In other words had they both lied? Well there is no doubt about it - they had.

Another very interesting point made by Mr Brown in his statement is that he says Carol rang him to warn him I was going to make a visit to his office. Surely if Mr Brown who is six foot six inches was afraid of me, he would have avoided the meeting and gone out until I had been and gone. The more I uncover, the more I wonder just how far I was being pressed to act in this silly predictable way. If that was the case, the plan worked wonderfully well.

After the attack Mr Brown says in his statement, and (yes I have a copy) that he left his own wife and children in 1985. He says, "I have not co-habitated with anyone. Nor am I at the moment." Blatant lies. He goes on to speak of Carol and myself by saying, "I believe both parties are living in rented accommodation." Carol was in a rented house just round the corner from his. Her sister used to mind Jonathan and David whilst they indulged in their love nest. He goes on to relate the day I called at his office, and surprise surprise! No Violet Mist, not even Scotch mist.

Mr Brown then says, "I started a relationship with Carol Armstrong in January 1990, having ended a relationship with someone else in December 1989." He of course omits that he was away with Carol in Tenerife in September. He tells the story of how Lee and I went along on that March morning, the 11th of March 1990.

Throughout this account he tries to avoid the fact he and Carol were together, but at no time does he mention the whereabouts of Jonathan and David, the children I had gone to visit.

In a follow up statement he says he handed over Carol's divorce details at the beginning of February 1990. He then goes on to report that on the 24th OF MAY 1990, he had the contract threat call *Hey Brown, I've got the contract on you. I'm gonna fucking wrap you up for good.*

Later, he says *I have been asked by the police if I am aware of any person, either relating to my personal or professional life, who may wish to harm or who would be responsible for the attack upon me of August 17th 1990. I know of no-one other than George Armstrong, because of previous threats he has uttered to me.*

So what about Terry Lyed? On May the 25th he had gone to Hoylake Police station and told officer Lonfurgoten the caller was Terry Lyed, Carol's cousin.

It seemed the whole case was based on shaky witnesses, tape recordings, idle threats and lies. One thing was very clear. Someone *had* attacked Mr Brown; it was indeed a vicious attack. The perpetrator should be caught and punished. Instead they seemed intent on pinning the blame firmly on me.

If I hadn't done it, I had arranged it.

Inspector Dorkins had said I had 'Underworld connections'. He might just as well have come into court and said, This man is guilty." The prosecution had pointed a finger at me and said,

YOU HIRED A HIT MAN.

****

CHAPTER TEN
THE HIT PARADE RECORDING

A TRIAL is a game of words. They shuffle them up and make black white and white black. Truth is offered, but truth is hidden and truth takes a hiding. This was like a boxing match of words. The trouble was my counsel was missing punches. The truth was having difficulty fighting back. It lay exhausted on the ropes, as I sat there listening - out for the count. Rigid, I looked into space, my mind starting to panic as the thought of prison seeped back into my mind. I had been on bail four months; I had tasted freedom. The thought of going back to prison truly frightened me. I prayed to God that that would not happen. I tried to keep my spirits but I started to fear the worst. I pushed my counsel; I told them they must bring out facts about Carol's behaviour and that my concern in the main had always been for Jonathan and David. I said the jury should be told about the two occasions when Carol threatened to commit suicide; in fact she had said she would kill herself and the children. Her words were that she was going to finish it all with herself and the boys. At the time I reported this to her doctor and the police and was gravely concerned. At the time she was staying in a small hotel in Southport and I was sick with worry.

I gave all this information to my solicitor, Mr Red, and my barrister, Mr White, but they said they could not use this information, as it would make the jury feel sorry for her. The same advice was given when I informed them that I had obtained information that Carol had also been involved in fraud, and that she had perpetrated various swindles on shops and credit card companies. She had used other names; she had after all obtained three driving licences, at a time she had not even passed a test! Incredibly, she fraudulently took out credit whilst I was away in prison. She actually used the address of my first wife to raise a loan. Lillian should have gone to the police about this, but then perhaps she had lost faith in them after what she had seen happen to me. Besides the Armstrong name was mud - the police and the press had seen to that. Still my counsel said, "No, keep quiet; it will only bring sympathy from the jury for her." How could this be? It was crazy - I was the victim and yet the truth about her could harm me.

I also informed Mr Red and Mr White that we now had proof that Terry Lyed had made the contract threat tape. Still they disregarded that fresh evidence and made no attempt to bring that to light. Nor did my counsel stop the contract threat from being played in court. To make things worse, when the jury retired they sent for the contract threat tape so they could hear it again. It's incredible isn't it? If it hadn't really happened, you would have thought all this was impossible. Well I can assure you it is all FACT. This charade of that trial and the first trial cost the British tax payer over ONE MILLION POUNDS and still they didn't get it right. What they actually did was JAIL AN INNOCENT MAN leaving the REAL ATTACKER OUT THERE.

Fear began to knot in my stomach. Here I was being tried for a supposedly crime of passion. Thoughts of being locked up made me shiver, the waste of life, the degradation, the injustice. My life had been so very different before all this. I had made a success of my business life. I had been   married for 36 years with a wonderful family, but then mid-life had somehow flawed me. I had fallen for a young woman. I'm not the first man or the last this will happen to. It's part of life - sometimes it works out. It didn't for me. The words ran through my head, 'There's no fool like an old fool'. I had made my choices and walked the road to ruin.

Thank God in all this mid-life madness I did make some right moves. For a start I left my first wife and family financially secure. I signed everything over to them. For all I have done wrong in life, I hope my children always remember that. I did it out of love and respect for Lil and my children. Though they may still have bad feelings about what I did, I hope that as they grow older, they will learn to forgive.

All these thoughts raced through my head. What would happen to Lee if they sent me back to prison? What would Carol and Roy Brown tell Jonathan and David about me? I just didn't know what to think about first, it was all so hopeless.

My mind drifted in and out of the court. I could not understand why my counsel had not used witnesses and evidence that would have surely gone in my favour. I thought about the statement Carl Eaden's wife had made, a statement which would have painted a very different picture of Carol. A portion of that statement reads:

I have known Carol and George Armstrong for about eight years.

I have been friends with Carol Armstrong but not particularly close. But when we got closer we used to go up to lunch at their home, and in the winter of 1989, it would be about October, I remember Carol confiding in me that she was seeing another man, even though she was living with George. She told me he bought her perfume.

It continues: *Carol said he writes me letters. In fact, she showed me a card where it says 'If the time is right and when the time is right, we'll be together' and a verse followed.*

Sandra Eaden then goes on to say after she had shown me the letter and card,

I asked her, 'Why did you go with George in the first place?' She then answered by saying that when she first met George, his sons even asked her out. But she said, 'Why have the small fry when you can have the big fish?'

I smiled to myself - some Big Fish I was! Well she certainly had landed me good and proper. Now she wanted me stuffed and nailed to the wall.

As the prosecution reeled me in for her, I struggled in advised silence, choked with the hook of emotion. They even brought up my war medals, God only knows why. I had explained that I had come by them by being so young and being in the right, or some would say wrong place, at the right time.

I said to him, "Are you trying to embarrass me? Do you think I'm telling lies?" He didn't say anything in answer to that.

But the thing that really got up the prosecution's nose was the fact I would not look at the photographs taken by the police of the injuries suffered by Mr Brown. I flatly refused to look at them.

I told the prosecution, "No! I will not look at them; they are nothing to do with me and I don't see why I should look at them."

Still he persisted in his questioning of me. It went on for several hours. Then it was the turn of my defence. Mr White my barrister approached the Judge saying he had a legal technicality to discuss and would the judge kindly retire the jury for several minutes whilst they discussed this. The Judge did so, suggesting the jury take time for a break and perhaps a cup of tea. Then Mr White said that he had a witness he wanted to produce. Immediately the prosecution jumped up and objected strongly. The witness was in fact Mrs Kemp who had come forward to give evidence for me. After all kinds of legal discussions and arguments regarding Mrs Kemp, the Judge simply refused to allow Mrs Kemp to speak. He agreed with the prosecutor that it would only go to the credit of Mrs Armstrong. How on earth could it go to the credit of Mrs Armstrong? Mrs Kemp's evidence without doubt would have proved my wife had been involved with several men prior to the attack on Mr Brown. Mrs Kemp could confirm she had been with another man the night before Mr Brown was attacked. Mrs Kemp was in no doubt of my innocence and was prepared to come forward despite personal threats. Her courage was however to no avail. They would not let her appear.

The jury were then returned to the court room and the trial continued.

My barrister now proceeded to put my case to the jury. Within this period the alarm bell went in the court room. Because of this, the whole court was advised to evacuate the building. It was bedlam really; we all had to make our way down the main staircase to the main entrance. Several hundred of us were there, including as always now, the reporting media, be they press, radio or television. It seems there had been a bomb scare. We stood there and, as we did so, we could see several groups of people being led out and escorted away. These in fact were jury members being taken to nearby hotels. Mr White indicated that me and members of my family should take a short step to a nearby restaurant for coffee, where Mr Red also joined us. Whilst there we had some lunch and talked over various points of the trial.

At about two o'clock we were all invited back into the building. No-one was quite sure why the alarm had gone off, or in fact what had really transpired. But there we were - back in Court Five on floor five, a place I will never forget as long as I live. I sat there, and listened as the Judge apologised for the delay and the problem of the alarm. Then he proceeded in his summing up. He spoke in legal terms, stressing certain points of law and facts of the case. I blinked, I swallowed. I locked my hands together. What else could I do? My heart beat like a rock in my chest, and panic ran through my veins as my eyes looked around at the rows of faces. Faces that all eventually would look my way. They would all want to look at me, the man who had HIRED A HIT MAN. That is what they had been told, and it must be true as the press had told them. I can't ever really describe what I was feeling that day. I think I wished I was dead. This was like dying over and over again; my life was being taken away from me minute by minute, and this court-room hammered it home to me how little time I had left of my life.

I heard some of what the Judge said; some of it I frankly missed.

You do when you are frightened. I do however remember him saying to the jury that if they did not reach a decision they would have to go to a hotel for the weekend until they had reached a verdict. So now the jury retired, none of them I'm sure keen on being locked away in a hotel for the weekend.

We then went from the court room and decided what to do until the jury came back. Whilst there, we were informed that the jury had requested the contract threat tape. But this tape not only held the contract threat, it also featured my calls to Mr Brown made in March 1990. So the tape was already linking me to that contract threat. Surely my calls should have been presented on a separate tape? How was this edited tape allowed as evidence?

When I heard the jury had requested the tape, I knew it was clear they were relying on this to make a firm judgment.

My thoughts flew to Lee; he had been so upset these past few days. He had continually asked me, "What will happen to me Dad, if you go back to prison?". His mother had disowned him, and he was alone in the world without me. To my first family Lee was living proof I had left them for Carol. Poor Lee. God, my heart ached for him. Thank God he has survived through this heartache; he's worth all the pain I have suffered. I love you Lee. Don't ever forget that.

Thoughts of Lee now filled my mind. He'd lost all contact with Jonathan and David, and it seemed his mother intended to keep him from them indefinitely. Mr Brown could see his own children by his first marriage quite regularly. Why then could he not understand that I needed to see my boys? That Lee wanted to see his brothers? He had been very close to Jonathan before that fateful Christmas.

I then thought about that day Carol's father visited me with Carol's first husband. If only I could have grasped what they were saying. I now realized Carol was mentally disturbed, and she had a code of conduct that was based on lies and deceit. But she was also a beautiful and clever woman who could charm the birds from the trees.

I sat there with my family, a family I had left. Still they had faith in me. I looked at Mark my youngest, his face trying to stay brave. I gave him my wallet and chain along with my watch and ring. I told him to keep these with him in case things went against me. I also arranged for Mrs Smith to go along to the school and collect Lee. My brother Lawrence said he would collect our pet dogs from their home. These things had to be discussed, for there would be no time for making arrangements if the jury found me guilty.

Now it was time to go back inside the court. We were told the jury was ready. My heart turned over and I said my goodbyes and kisses to my family. I trembled; we were all upset. If it went badly for me I would not see them again that day. Our eyes met; some tried to smile; then silently we parted.

Back in the court room we waited as things were organised. Carol who was still legally my wife sat there holding hands with Mr Brown. Nearby another gentleman friend of Carol's also enjoyed this farce. Another recent conquest who Mrs Kemp had said Carol had seduced. Now it seemed he had assigned all his legal work to Roy Brown. But still I could say nothing. Just how deep this slime was they were all wading in, I don't know. Maybe I will never know. One thing was crystal clear. I was now paying dearly for my fatal attraction to a woman who clearly wanted me out of the way for good.

The jury in place, the court now quiet, the judge entered from his chambers and took his seat. The clerk of the court stood up. I held my breath; there was a feeling everyone else had too. The clerk then said.

"Would the foreman please stand? Mr Foreman, please answer my first question either 'Yes' or 'No'. Has the jury reached a verdict upon which you are all agreed?"

The foreman of the jury then replied.

147

"Yes".

The clerk of the court asked, "Do you find the defendant guilty or not guilty ?"

The foreman answered, "Guilty."

The clerk of the court asked, "You find the defendant guilty and that is the verdict of you all?"

The foreman nodded and replied, "It is."

The clerk of the court then said, "Thank you."

I was stunned beyond belief. I shouted out, "Why? I've done nothing wrong. Why? Why? I'm not guilty."

I heard my brother call out, "If this is British justice, it stinks! It's shit! This man is innocent!"

I broke down crying. The officer alongside me held my arm and said, "George sit down."

The court had erupted. The judge spoke loudly asking for silence. I looked over at Mr Brown who had now thrown his arms in the air and then put them around Carol. He laughed and grinned at me. I looked back a broken man.

Then I shouted, "I suppose now you are both happy."

They just grinned back. The Judge then spoke, proceeding with the sentence.

"George Armstrong, you have been found guilty of the offence of conspiracy to cause grievous bodily harm."

Tired of being silenced I spoke again, "I haven't done anything."

The Judge went on to say this.

This court appreciates from what it has heard that you may have been provoked by your wife's behaviour. It may be that she acted in a way towards you that was wholly unjustified. You have suffered the dreadful experience of a broken marriage. You have been beset by business problems. You are a man, as I indicated to

the jury, who might fairly be treated as one of previous good char-
acter. The testimonials that have been put before the court echo
that view. You have a son, three children in fact, but particularly
Lee, the one who evidently is particularly attached to you, a son
of whom you may be proud. The fact he can write the touching
letter to the court as he has done doing the best for his father; this
child of whom you will be proud and are entitled always to con-
tinue to be proud. It is highly unlikely that anything that happens
to you here today is going to impair his affection for you.

It is, however, the fact that this court has to regard you as one
who has indulged yourself in a frenzy of hate. You have become
involved in a course of conduct that had near-fatal results. You
have shown yourself in all these circumstances as a man who has
become highly dangerous. This court has a duty to protect the
public. The sentence has to reflect the fact that the court is deter-
mined to protect the public from a man who may be dangerous.
The sentence of this court is that you go to prison for seven years.
Take him down.

Silent for too long, I shouted again. "This is ridiculous. I
haven't done anything. What do you say of her boyfriends?" Again
someone called.

"If that is English justice, it's shit."

Then I called out again, "I have done nothing."

Once more someone called, "Stick it right there, it's shit. It
stinks - that is all I can say."

People now started to leave the court whilst I was put in handcuffs and taken down below. Soon I was in a cell, alone.

My whole being horror-struck by what had happened to me.
Words and faces flashed through my mind as I sat there shaking.
After several minutes an officer came to me and said, "George,
come this way."

I went with him to a room where my defence counsel waited for
me. Mr White, my barrister, indicated they would make an appeal

immediately. Mr Red nodded in agreement. I listened, my spirit crushed by these events. There was then a short conversation They shook my hands and left. They had said words like, "Try not to worry too much." But I was still too stunned to react to such trite and feeble words. How the hell could I not worry? I had been sentenced for seven years in prison for a crime I knew nothing about. I had a son out there who would be breaking his heart. My world had been flushed down the toilet. "Try not to worry" was a poor choice of words. But poor choices of words had ruined us all. Me first with my foolish calls to Roy Brown - words said in anger. They, my legal advisors, had not said enough words, they had not fought hard enough. I had time to go over that trial time and time again, and each time I cursed them for not presenting evidence and witnesses they had at hand. I began then to ask myself if they really were on my side? Did they ever really think I was an innocent man? Or were they just playing the legal game with me as pawn?

As if in a trance, I was returned to the cell. Later I was taken to a visitors' room where my family waited to see me. Also there was Mrs Smith. The feeling in that room was dreadful; no one could comprehend what had happened. Thick impregnable glass sliced me away from them. I was now cut off from the world, distanced from all that was freedom. I looked at this sorry group, made victims by knowing me. Their love, their kindness was making them suffer with me. It was unbearable for us all. Severed, we could not touch, it was cruel and inhuman. We said little, it was all too upsetting and soon I had to leave, waving goodbye as the door was closed on them. Back again to that cell I went. Seven years hammering on my every thought. Seven years! Seven years! it repeated in my head over and over again. How in God's name could it be right? I hadn't done anything. I was an innocent man. Seven years! Seven years! it pounded in my head, and each time it went round I grew angrier and more upset. How could the jury have got it so wrong? What evidence had there been that I had done this? But I couldn't think straight. I was tortured with thoughts of the living hell of prison life.

My mind wandered back to memories of Walton Jail. The smell of the place, the madness of some of the inmates. The crimes that existed within prisons themselves. I would die, I was sure of it. How could I possibly survive? I was an old man by prison standards. It would kill me off. If I was honest at that moment I wanted to do nothing else but lie down and die. If there had not been Lee out there, needing my love, having faith in me, maybe I would have given up.

As it was Lee and all my fine boys, and daughters deserve more. I was going to have to fight for my life and the truth. In my children I found the courage to drag myself back from hell. But that would be a long road to travel. For now I felt I was finished. Finished good and proper. I cried. I thought of Carol. How could she have done this to me? She surely knew I was not the guilty party. I wiped a tear away, and I thought of the luxury life we had enjoyed.

My thoughts turned to how she had changed, how she had deceived me. Perhaps she wanted to hurt me like this because it had been me who had requested the divorce? Maybe this was her way of punishing me. If it was, then it was a cruel hatred. She knew in cutting me down she would break Lee's heart. I thought about our age difference - she had been so young when we met, me being thirty years her senior. None of that mattered in those early days, and of course the children kept me young. My eyes then welled as I thought of Jonathan and David. The two boys she had not let me see for so long. Now they had been taken away from me forever.

'Try not to worry,' ran through my mind. Words of comfort - such poor compensation for my loss of liberty. I shook my head in hopelessness. 'There would be an appeal' a small voice called to me from a place inside my head. But a louder voice called back. 'It's no use, I've had it.'

Sitting there I waited for the key in the lock. Eventually I heard the familiar sound and the door opened. I was handcuffed, taken outside and handcuffed to another prisoner. Then we were led out to a coach parked outside the courts. The grim and certain reminder that I was now heading back to Walton Jail.

We sat there joined together by steel. Man to man, the coach was full. I couldn't speak. There was no energy left in me. My mind one minute was blank, the next it filled to burst. Tears, anger, fear, desolation, are only words of feelings. No-one can ever describe the feelings I had. No one could relate the strange place my mind became that day. Faith and hope I had seen destroyed. As for Charity, well, that lived in those who cared for me and in my true friends. Truth, justice. For me they had become two dirty words. Once I had believed in them. I, like most people, thought the truth will out. Well I had learnt a big lesson. Lies can out-box the truth; they had, they had won hands down.

Dusk was falling as the coach moved away. I was pleased for it shaded my eyes that were sore. There were others too glad of the dark. We travelled through the city along the Dock Road, up along Commercial Road towards the Princess Bingo Club. I knew this route so well. I had travelled this way whilst on remand in Walton Jail. Soon we were at Melrose Road; I could see the Princess, my special Princess. My heart ached as we passed by. Within no time we were at the gates of Walton Jail; they opened and the coach moved from life into my living death.

Once more dignity was taken from us as we were stripped and all our belongings were taken from us. I walked nude into the shower as did the other men. When I had finished, I was directed to a window where I was issued clothing. This time my clothing was that of a convicted prisoner. On remand you are issued with a different uniform so that it is clear what type of prisoner you are. Next I was issued with bedding. After this procedure I was taken to the convicted prisoners' wing. Next I was examined by a doctor, and again I was asked if I was suicidal. What else was there to feel? This was going to be a living death for me. Here I was amongst all kinds of prisoners, men from all walks of life. Hard men, cruel men. Some victims themselves. Mad men, twisted sly men. If they could see you were an independent man, they did their best to try and break your spirit. These men tell lies about you. They create problems and situations around you, their aim, always to be disruptive. Such men are the flames in your own private hell. Men who foster hatred, men who foster grudges and deal out pain to others. Men who foster favouritism of officers and lie about you to them. Men who seek strange alliances at the first kind word or deed. In this world you lived your time on a knife edge, never knowing who was friend of foe until the last.

There were those who treated prison like a home, sad souls who had found crime their career. These men had hardened to the life. Me, well I was devastated. How was I here amongst this sorry ragbag of human nature? Then I looked at these prison officers, just as much prisoners as we were. Only our uniforms separated us. They were men trying to do an honest day's work, and their job was not an easy one, not by any stretch of the imagination.

Down I was taken to the lower ground. There I was locked in my own cell. The low light looked as lifeless and depressed as I felt. I shuddered - it was very cold in there. But even colder were the hours that passed as my mind went over the day. Lee filled my thoughts; I could see his lovely face horror-struck on hearing the news his Dad would not be coming home. I cried as I lived it. My poor, poor Lee. I just prayed to God they wouldn't tell him I had been sentenced to seven years' imprisonment. We had just organised our home in Magull and were settled in. Lee was attending school there. This now would all have to change; he would be forced to go back to the life he had had before. I cried bitterly as I still do. I see that little boy all alone,and it broke my heart as I knew it would break his. His mother had locked him out of her life; her thoughts had been only for herself and her new life. Now she could stand back and watch us both being punished. But what in God's name for? I was innocent. And Lee was just a child, but still he too was being punished by this wrongful conviction against me. If Carol had any kindness in her she would have gone to Lee now, she would have given solace to her eldest boy. She knew, more than anyone, how alone that boy was.

But no, he remained locked out. A prisoner of circumstance and a mother who would always hold his heart to ransom. Because after all is said and done, she is his mother and always will be. Lee loves her, she knows that.

As tears of anguish flooded my eyes, my mind jumped from scene to scene of my own horror story. The lies, the press headlines. The jury sending for the tape-recording of the contract threat. The faces of my family, my barrister's words, 'Try not to worry'.

Then I thought about the appeal, and I started to wonder how long it would take. If only my defence had produced evidence that would have proved Carol had other men who could be jealous of her association with Brown. If only they had called Mrs Kemp. The 'if onlys' haunted the dark like shadows.

Not satisfied with their rough justice, Carol and Roy celebrated my conviction in the Café Bar in Southport that very evening. Carol had arranged this bash. Obviously confident of the outcome of my trial. This the very place where outside she had said to me, "I've got one I can't get rid of now," - meaning Brown of course. Little did he know what a fool she had played us all for. But he will learn.

So whilst my poor Lee sobbed that night, his mother drank champagne and laughed. I think this speaks for itself.

****

CHAPTER ELEVEN
SENT DOWN BUT NOT OUT

MORNING crept in my cell. The door was slung open and we were told to slop out. There was no toilet here. We used a bucket. After that we were given tea and toast. Next we were led to another place, lined up and became a queue to meet the Governor.

The night before a prisoner had told me I would be moved to another prison. He said being a long term prisoner, they would move me out. I listened and nodded. It just sounded like another part of hell to me. What did I care where I would be? I couldn't be with Lee, I couldn't give a damn where I was. We tramped along the shuffling line, each with our own story to tell. Then it came to my turn.

Defeated, condemned I looked back at success I had known. There, opposite me sat a man who knew who and where he was in life. He felt secure, he knew he would be home soon, free to enjoy his family, his life, his freedom. They were things we all take for granted. If someone had told me, say three years before, that I would be here like this, I would have laughed. The thought would have been ludicrous, madness. I would have said, it can't happen. Looking at this man, I now was all too aware how very easily it can happen.

We talked and the Governor told me that being the age I was, I would be moved to another wing. I made no comment. I didn't really care about anything anymore. When the meeting was over, I trudged to my cell but later that morning I was moved to another wing. I was then introduced to the cleaning officer who found me a cell which I would share with another prisoner. Then after a short time I was taken away for an interview. This turned out to be a job interview. I was told I was now a cleaner and that my job would be mopping the floors which included the area of the toilets.

That morning I also filled in an application form for a visiting pass. This was to enable one of my family, or my friends Mr and Mrs Smith who had taken in Lee, to visit me. The visit would be a world away - I would have to wait until next week. A day can seem endless in prison, and the thought of a week was awful to me. But then what had I to tell them? My humiliation was complete. I was now cleaning prison toilets. What more could they do to me?

As the day went on, I recognised faces I had seen here before. Men whom I had met when I had been held here on remand. Faces I would have preferred not to have seen again looked over to me. Then came the calls, *Mafia Godfather*, and word soon went around that I had hired a hit man. I felt eyes follow me, some challenging, some tinged with fear. Eyes, whispers seemed to follow me all day. Mafia Godfather cleaning the toilets - somehow I don't think the two go together. Surely if I was this heavy they had made me out to be, I would have made sure I was treated better than this. But no, there were those in there who would believe anything. And why not? A jury had judged me guilty, and by doing so had said, "Yes, all the press are right. This man is all these things, he must be." But in this captive world, my title would prove a curse and a blessing.

Within that day I was also called to the appeals office.

On arrival I was informed that my barrister had appealed for me. I was then asked to sign the necessary documents so that it could proceed. I was eager now. Some morsel of hope had been thrown to me like a bone to a dog. I would sit and chew on that bone, bury it in my soul and when my spirit felt very low, I would dig it out again and worry it. "All I had to do was wait," they said. I would be given a date for my appeal. I waited, and waited and it did eventually come. That appeal was to come eighteen months later. Months I can never have again, lost crucial months with a son who needed me. I had been a foolish man, and I had said foolish things but I had not committed a crime. Putting me in this place was a crime and I knew who were the guilty ones who had made sure I was placed there. For Lee and all my children and for myself, I will make sure those people are faced with their crime. If I am dead or alive, the truth will be told. Those who have lied will tell the truth, those who have remained silent in duplicity will speak up. The guilty will be flushed out.

So the days and nights passed, and every evening I wrote a letter to Lee. I also wrote many times to the good people who had taken him in, Mr and Mrs Smith. I was so thankful he was in their safe hands, I am eternally grateful to them for helping Lee and me in this way. Not many would have been so selfless in this matter.

I thought of my other children too, the girls and boys I had fathered with my first wife Lillian. I knew my leaving them and their mother had hurt them badly, but they had still shown their love for me. I wept bitterly for so many regrets. Then there was poor little Jonathan and David; they had been thrown from pillar to post. They had a Daddy that loved them, but that was not enough for me to hold onto them. I held my head in my hands. I tortured myself trying to come to terms with the past I had created and a future leading only to a cold grave.

I hoped the children of my first marriage would understand that I had always worked hard and done my very best to give them a better start in life. I had worked long, long hours in my quest for success. I had travelled, sometimes not being there for them, when I should have been. But that is life. I don't claim to have been the perfect father. I do however claim and declare my love for them. I am also very proud of them and their children. For I am a grandfather to eleven children. Thoughts too haunted me about the two babies I had never seen, the children I had fathered in 1948 and 1949. I prayed their lives had turned out well and that they had flourished. These thoughts like waves ran to and fro in my mind, sometimes quiet and gentle but frequently crashing against the walls of my head. The pain of it all was too hard to bear.

In the next two weeks I had various visitors at the prison. Two of these were Mr Red and Mr Knight to discuss aspects of my appeal. I was still very disillusioned with everything, and at a very low ebb in life. The appeal seemed so very far away, and my mind was still firmly fixed on worrying for Lee.

I had banned Lee from coming to see me as I couldn't face seeing him there. I just didn't want this poor lad seeing me like this. But after a few weeks, I gave in. I had to - he wanted to see his Dad. On his first visit to Walton Jail, Lee became terribly upset. God, that was an awful day. The visit must have frightened him - he was only ten years old and it must have been terrifying for him. Brave lad that he was he couldn't hold back the tears. On that first visit Lee clung to my body. When it was time to leave he had to be prized away from me. Even when he had gone, I could still feel his grip on my body. His small imprinted form had moulded into mine. I watched and ached as he was taken away, his sobs the sentence this injustice had meted out to him. How could his mother leave him desolate like this? Surely she must have known how he would suffer. Lee, once at a private school, was now schooled in Kirkby. Those who know Liverpool accept that Kirkby is a tough area, and my son now had to get tough quickly to survive there. The children hounded him, bullied him. They called after him, "Your Dad's a murderer." His existence was no better than mine; we were both locked in situations neither of us could change. I both looked forward to and dreaded visits from Lee in equal measure. But the anguish of those visits was worth every second spent with him. Neither he nor I should have suffered like this, and I vowed in my heart I would prove my innocence. But how? Where would I start? I started to make notes, and from there, the idea of my book evolved, but there was a lot of time to get through before that.

As time passed, I was given another job within Walton - the

position being on labour control. I was pleased to get this job, as it gave me more time out of the cell. We were locked up for 23 hours a day remember, and so doing anything was better than being in that cell. My role was to walk around to various wings unaccompanied, making notes regarding the movements of prisoners. At the end of each landing there was a board which indicated which prisoner was in which cell. This board had to be kept up to date so that prison officers could locate these individuals. I also had to visit K wing where all the sexual offenders were located. These men had to be kept separate from other prisoners, as amongst them were child molesters who were considered the lowest of the low - which I agree with. They were kept separate for their own protection. If they had not been, most would have been done away with by other prisoners.

A highlight of life in Walton was being allowed to watch television three times a week. You could also change your clothes twice a week. Better still you could shower one, two or three times a week. Keeping and staying clean was a luxury. It helped me retain some small amount of dignity.

The mail too brought life into the prison. How I looked forward to that special link with the outside world! Believe it or not I even had two letters from Carol who was now legally my ex-wife. She said she would send me photographs of Jonathan and David. I also had letters from Carol's mother, Doris, in which she said that she had read one of my letters to Carol and she had broken down crying. This only can point to the fact that deep down, deep inside her, Carol was aware of the problems she had caused for me and the children.

During that time in Walton Jail, I had several visits from my sons. I also was visited by a very brave and wonderful lady - Lillian. My brother Lawrence also came to see me. The care I was shown by my family was incredible.

There were other visitors too who were not quite family anymore. Carol's sister April, wife of Terry Lyed, paid me a visit. It was on this visit that April informed me that it had been Terry who had made the contract threat call. The news of this was like salt in my wound, but, as it lay there smarting, I made sure that I would bring all this to light one day.

There was good news too, like the morning I was called to the Governor's office and told I would be moving to Kirkham open prison. The inmates had told me they would never let me go from Walton, and that I would have to do my seven years there. The thought was unbearable, and so when I was told I was going to Kirkham there was a glimpse of hope flickering in the very distant future.

When the time came to be moved to Kirkham, I reflected on the terrible time I had endured in Walton. I had met prisoners of crime and prisoners of conscience. Men of position and men of no standing at all. I recalled the MP who was there because of the poll tax dispute. There were also men who had been associated with Mr Hatton within the City of Liverpool office. All had a tale to tell, but the majority knew why they had been put there. I never had that consolation. I knew I had done nothing wrong.

I said my goodbyes to the men I had come to know there. I also thanked the prison officers for their assistance for they had been very considerate to me, and it was no fault of theirs I was there. Instinctively I had taken to work in the prison - as always I had striven for a better job there. It was in my blood; work was second nature to me.

As we approached reception, I was so thankful I was leaving this place. I had written and told everyone I was being moved to Kirkham, near Blackpool and they had all written back saying they were pleased for me. For the first time I felt a little lifted - things were moving on. As instructed I went to the counter to collect my civilian clothes. I was then told to go and change. I was emotional having my own clothes on my back. You just can't imagine this, but it's these small happenings that bring out the vulnerability within you.

Over the months me and my clothes had parted friends; they

160

looked like my clothes, but they hung on me. They felt big, as if made for some other chap. But then in a way they had. The person who had worn these clothes on arrival was not the same man any more. I had not only lost weight; I had lost my freedom.

In the reception area there were several other prisoners working, some giving out refreshments. I looked over at a prisoner who had made several passes at me whilst in Walton. He had made it blatantly clear he wanted sex with me, and I had found the whole scene in there very unhealthy and distasteful. This particular man was very effeminate, and I felt his mannerisms uncomfortable. It was all very embarrassing. There were many homosexual men in Walton and it was wise to make it clear early on that you were not 'gay'. Some would not take a rebuff too kindly, and there were some very tough guys amongst that group. I did my best to avoid their company.

I don't have any problem with gay people; I have nothing whatsoever against them. But in a place like prison that you have to set your guide lines up swiftly, and let people know where they stand with you. Any sign of weakness is used against you, any strength is constantly challenged. Being older had its very small advantages, and there weren't many of those in that place.

So we nodded our goodbyes. I also shook hands with some officers. No handcuffs were used for this move and I felt the whole thing far more humane. As I walked out to the coach, I looked back, and I felt sorry for anyone who, like me, was innocent. I also had nothing but sympathy for those poor officers having to work in such a place.

Climbing on board the coach, we were allowed to choose our own seat and this morsel of freedom was like being given the coach itself. There were about eighteen of us travelling to Kirkham. The atmosphere was relaxed and there was an air of hope blowing through my lungs, or maybe it was just getting out of the stench of the place. The coach moved off and we cruised down to the large gates. They were opened, and we travelled along Walton road and headed for the M6 motorway. It seemed no time at all before we were on route for Kirkham. As the signs indicated directions to Blackpool, my mind recalled brighter memories of this route. I told myself this was the beginning of my road to freedom. I knew I had to keep strong and fight on. As my mind planned ahead the hum of the coach was comforting. It was taking me forward, nearer to my appeal date. I looked about me and the men with me looked happier. Then as I gazed at the fields we passed, I day-dreamed as the sun moved across them. This was a little bit of heaven to me and no-one could stop me enjoying it.

Somebody mentioned it was Wednesday. I nodded in agreement. I knew only too well what day it was. It was the 21st of August 1991. There had been very few days to remember these past months. How could I forget this one.

Kirkham, I had been told, was originally an RAF aerodrome. So it was in keeping that the reception area was situated in a Nissan hut. As we moved nearer the hut, I could see prisoners walking about, none of them with escorts. I couldn't believe it, nor could some of the other men. None of us had any idea of what an open prison was really like. I don't think we believed it was going to be anything like the officials had described. But here we were, and so far, it looked okay.

After the normal formalities and the usual paperwork, we were issued with the prison uniform which was quite different from what we had been used to. We were given a shirt and slacks but saved the horror of the prison boot. Here we could wear our own shoes. For me this was a blessing.

From that point we were interviewed by various personnel and then shown to our own particular quarters. From there we were taken on a tour of the prison which took in the cinema, the gymnasium - there was even a pond where you could actually go fishing. I was staggered, as was a chap I had made friends with on the journey to Kirkham. Bill was a restaurant owner from West Derby Road. Bill was in prison for tax evasion. To remind you, as I have

162

mentioned before, there are all kinds of people in prison. Not all prisoners were die-hard convicted criminals.

Some men were in there for non-payment of tax, driving offences, arguments. But sadly all these men were thrown in prison alongside some of life's professional criminals - murderers too, not to mention sex offenders. It was crazy. Why mix all these men like this?

The murderers and sex criminals were there to re-adjust - sometimes before their impending release. You frequently never knew who these men were; you just had to mingle. But that was the downside of Kirkham you had to accept; you had no choice in the matter. To me it seems wrong that people on appeal should have to mix with men like that. Why should someone who has refused to pay a poll tax bill be forced to share a room with someone who has killed someone in cold blood? Why should anyone have to sleep alongside a child sex offender? I feel this part of the system is very wrong indeed.

It does not take much imagination to realize that disturbances are bound to erupt. When a child offender was uncovered there were always arguments that would end in a fight, often a wounding. For the disturbed mind of the murderer, this was a great excuse to cause injury. For the sane, it was an abomination that would often drive them to physical violence. Being in close proximity to such a mix of evil is bound to rub off and cause hostility in men. It was not surprising that prisoners were often being moved around and some even moved out.

But all that was to come, on that special August summer day when I found hope again.

Our meal that evening was marvellous, and afterwards, Bill, my new pal, loaned me his phone card so that I could ring Lee. Phone cards were like gold in prison, the phone being the only real contact with the outside. I constantly wrote to my son, but there was nothing like hearing his voice on the line.

Like everyone there I queued for the chance to make a call. When I got through I broke down and cried. So did Lee. I was not alone; there were many other men who cried when using the phone. Your emotions are locked up with you, but they soon break free when you hear voices of a loved one.

I looked forward to those calls so much, they kept me going when my spirit drifted low. For Lee, well his Dad may not have been there for him, but he knew more than ever how much he meant to me. I was so proud of that brave boy.

For Carol and Roy Brown, life was very different now. They had become celebrities; they were of course the couple in the famous *Hit Man Trial*. So when they married on August the 31st 1991, once again they were featured in several newspapers. The *Liverpool Echo* gave them a splendid write up and photo. The headline read: WEDDING JOY ENDS A YEAR OF SADNESS. It actually says in that write-up:

Carol, a mother of three first met Mr Brown when she instructed him to begin divorce proceedings.

It also says they were going to the Caribbean for their honeymoon. Still the circus rolled on, and I was the clown they had locked in the cage.

I read the headlines; I shook my head. It was beyond all understanding. Once we had been that happy couple. Now I sat in prison, convicted of attempted murder. It would have been easy to throw in the towel if Lee had not needed me.

Kirkham certainly was not a place to sit around and feel sorry for yourself. Besides, I am a compulsive worker and within no time at all I was back at work again.

The Governor asked me if I could use a cash till. I was amazed at this, and I quickly answered yes.

He said, "Right, you go to the veg shop."

I was puzzled at first, but soon discovered the popular Kirkham fruit and veg shop was within the prison, and that the produce sold there was from the farm where the prisoners worked. There was a good selection offered: tomatoes, potatoes, carrots, onions, apples - the usual variety of fare you would see in any local high street. The produce is of course also used for the prisoners' meals. The other quota is then sold to the civilians who work in the prison service at Kirkham. I felt very privileged being given a job like this. I wore the blue prison shirt, a collar and tie, and felt so much better working in these surroundings. The people who came in were very nice, and I used to be able to have a cup of tea now and then. It was very good for me that job.

But now came another body blow. Not content that I was locked away from all that I loved, Roy Brown now took it upon himself to cause me further problems in Kirkham. I was called to the Governor's office for a meeting with the Deputy governor. At this meeting he advised me that it would be better if I stopped writing to Doris Grey. I was bewildered with this request. I always remained on good terms with Doris. Whilst I had been away, her letters had kept me in touch with Jonathan and David. She had also given me much assistance in my search for the truth. I asked the Deputy what this was all about. He told me he had received a letter from Mr Brown, via his solicitor's office, saying that my letters were upsetting Doris, and that I should stop writing to her. I was dumb-struck by this news - it was too ridiculous for words. I just couldn't believe it. I told the Governor that there must be some mistake. I would never cause distress to Doris. Why on earth would I want to do that? The Governor said he would write to Doris and sort things out. True to his word he did. This is what he said.

Dear Mrs Grey

I am in receipt of a letter dated 29 August 1991 from Mr R B Brown of Smethers Warpole & Smethers (solicitors) stating that the letters you have been receiving from George Armstrong (DT3295) have been causing you 'distress and upset'. Mr Brown asked me to ensure you received no further communications from Mr Armstrong. Consequently I interviewed Mr Armstrong and obtained his undertaking not to write to you again. However in view of the fact that he continues to receive mail from you, I must now ask you to confirm in writing whether or not Mr Brown's request is in accord with your wishes.

Yours sincerely

G Bowater

Deputy Governor

This letter was dated the 4th of September. The letter from Brown was dated the 31st of August, the day Roy and Carol were married. Was this one final attempt to sever me from his new mother-in-law? Doris replied to the Governor. She also wrote to me. I have a copy here; it reads:

Dear George,

I was amazed to receive a letter today from Mr Bowater your Deputy Governor. I have just replied to it. I have said your letters have never caused me any distress and upset and the letter from the solicitors was written without my knowledge.

Sincerely,

Doris.

Roy Brown had told lies about me in the past - they had gone unnoticed. This small but foolish lie made him look very discredited in such a petty way. Thankfully this time the lie did not work. Doris and I still kept in touch.

As soon as I could I applied for a V.O. (Visiting Order), and arranged for Lee to visit me. I had written to Lee and Mr and Mrs Smith who would be accompanying him. I was full of praise for Kirkham and said that I was feeling much more encouraged with things. I was so glad in my heart that Lee no longer had to visit

Walton Jail.

This visit took place at the end of August and I must say that visit was a happier one. We all seemed to smile more, the surroundings were so much better than the other place I had endured. But sad to say, come leaving time Lee once again broke down and cried; he became upset and then so did I. It just couldn't be helped. We were both so full of the pain that all this had brought upon us.

That pain of loss burned in me. Losing the closeness of Lee hurt the most. I was doing my best to cope with this confinement. I knew there would come an end to it, and I prayed to God there would be.

Lee's tears were bitter, and they made me more determined than ever to ensure my appeal would succeed. Constant as I was in this effort, I soon talked the appeal over with the assistant Governor at Kirkham. At this meeting I met others who were also waiting for their appeals to come through. One man I met there would later, over the next weeks, have his come through. He went down to London, had his appeal heard and never returned. I was puzzled and queried this point with a prison officer. He explained that if you were successful with your appeal, you never came back. I was thrilled to hear this news. I was positive about my appeal and knew that when my turn came, I too would not be coming back.

Elation and joy were feelings rarely felt in Kirkham. You had to make the most of any good feelings you had. I was luckier than many. I not only had young Lee, I had a whole grown-up family. Sons and daughters who cared about their Dad. My sons, Gary and Lawrence, not only were there for me, they often put their hand in their pockets and helped financially. So did my ex-wife Lil; many would have turned their back, but not my Lil. She is a very special lady who, thank God, has forgiveness in her heart. So all in all, I had a lot going in my favour, and for the sake of those who loved me, and bore my name, I knew I must fight on to clear this stigma from me and the family.

It would now take another seventeen long months before my

appeal would be heard. Seventeen difficult months. Hope sometimes was shattered. Life on occasions was hard to bear. Kirkham was a whole lot better than Walton could ever be, but it was still a prison.

One good thing about Kirkham was the fact I was allowed a day out. This meant I could go home. Yes, home for a day! I was over the moon with this news. At once I set the ball rolling and arranged to go down and see Lee.

When the day arrived, I was so excited by it all. In the morning Mr and Mrs Smith picked me up; it all seemed like a dream. It felt strange - one minute I was locked away, the next free as a bird. It was marvellous to be out like that. I savoured every moment of every hour. I had a wonderful time with Lee. We walked together, talked about the future and the air bubbled with prospect of my release. It was hard for Lee to understand the long wait for my appeal. All he wanted to know was when his Dad would be coming home. I told him soon, and in my heart I prayed it would be so. My health was never good whilst I was in gaol. My heart had been broken; it held together with old memories that just wouldn't let it stop beating.

I also went over to see Lillian that day; it was a nice meeting. We had coffee, talked over things and I knew I had been blessed in knowing her. Before I left she gave me some toiletries to take back with me. Soap, toothpaste, things like that. I was very touched by this gesture.

I had several 'day-out' visits whilst in Kirkham and they were wonderful days of freedom that I cherished.

In Kirkham itself I found myself promoted. I was now given a job in the timber shop. Within that unit was a canteen for all the officers who worked there. My job was organising the rest room for them, making tea and just making sure things were okay. I also met civilians in this workshop, and so I found the job placement quite acceptable. The fruit and veg shop had been fine, but change in a prison is inevitable and often healthy. There were privileges too. The officers would give you the odd biscuit and you did have a little more freedom.

That's what life had come to, I thought. Being given a biscuit was a privilege. I had been a millionaire; I had owned property. I had controlled staff. I had been a successful man. Now here I was happy for crumbs off the table. My life had been turned inside out. Thankfully I had not turned bitter. It seemed I still had faith in the good in people and found some happiness in sharing.

Days turned, the evenings came and each night I used the phone. I was also in contact with Doris Grey who used to tell me how Jonathan and David were keeping, I missed the boys so much. When I was arrested that fateful day, I had in my pocket Jonathan's dummy. The last time his mother took him from me I had, in the upset, forgotten to give it to her. I kept it there - that dummy went to the prison with me. It is in fact written down on the list of personal items. I still have that dummy, and I treasure it. I even have clothing that once covered his little form. I love those little bones; I held them so many times.

But Doris had other things to tell me too, things I could hardly believe. Whilst on the telephone one evening, Doris mentioned that she had spoken to Carol on the previous day. She had said to her mother, "George won't get an appeal." I was staggered when I heard this. I was after all living every day for my chance at getting an appeal.

I said, "What do you mean? How do they know?"

She told me she didn't know, and repeated, "All Carol said was 'George won't get an appeal.' "

I swallowed hard, my mouth went dry. Roy Brown was a solicitor, and he obviously was doing all in his power to stop me for gaining my freedom. But why? Shouldn't he have been more concerned about who his attacker had been? What was crazy is that he must have known this 'Hit Man' theory was a bit far-fetched. Or maybe someone did set him up. One thing is certain - it was never me. The police checked all my bank accounts, went through all my papers in order to find some amount of money I had taken out to pay the phantom Hit Man. They couldn't find anything, simply because there was nothing to uncover.

After that call, my spirits sank again. I was sure Roy Brown was pulling strings again and I was the puppet that was tangled in the wires of deception.

On November 31st 1991, a Thursday, three days later, I was called to the Governor's office. The Governor told me that my appeal had been turned down. They were not going to allow it. I must have turned white, I was so shocked. I then broke down. This news was unbearable, the appeal was vital to me. I felt in a life or death situation, and the thought of dying in a cell in jail horrified me. The officer aware of my distress tried to reassure me.

He said, "Write straight away and appeal again."

He went on to say it would take a little longer but I could try again. Distraught I nodded. I felt finished. I now knew that Roy Brown's influence as a solicitor was still working against me. How could I break free of his circle of contacts?

When I had regained my composure, I went to the library and obtained books on the subject of appeals procedure. At first I was disillusioned and thought I would not stand a chance. But soon I seemed to be making headway and in working at it, I grew a little more confident. From there I requested the forms to make a second application for my appeal hearing. When I received them, I studied them carefully. When they had been filled in and completed, they were sent off to the Lord Chief Justice of England in London.

****

CHAPTER TWELVE
LETTERS AFTER MY GOOD NAME

CHRISTMAS was a particularly bad time for me. This was my second spent in prison. I still couldn't believe it. If I had known I was still going to be locked up a year after that first dreadful Christmas in Walton Jail, I think I would have gone mad. Sometimes it is best we can't see over the horizon. I was sure I would not be found guilty because I was innocent, but here I was. It was hard for me, but harder for Lee.

His mother, and her new husband were still headline news it seemed. A Daily Post exclusive takes up half a page. The headline says: HUSBAND WHO HIRED HIT MAN REACHES OUT FROM PRISON. Then in much larger print it says: **COUPLE UNDER CLOUD OF HATRED.** The poor suffering couple are pictured under a Christmas tree; they are both laughing. Never are they seen with the children. Our son, Carol's son, my son, has the pain of reading this. He is in care with a family. I am in prison.

The story reads, another fairy story, that I had bombarded them with letters and was contacting them by telephone. These calls, 'mysterious' they called them, were the kind where the phone rings, you pick it up and then it clicks off. The article once again mentions my *frenzy of hate*. The press seemed to love these words. What amazes me is that not one of them could have asked to see these phantom letters. There **were** no letters, nor did I call them. The telephone in Kirkham was naturally monitored. If I had made these calls, I would have been stopped.

They go on to say that they have contacted the Governor of Kirkham asking him not to allow George Armstrong to send any more mail. When the governor read that article, he said, "Who are these people?" Who indeed.

But this feature was deliberate, as most of their publicity had been in the past. Now I feel this was their attempt at making sure any chance of appeal would be shaky. They were trying to say that I was still active in causing them distress - just as they did in Channel 4's *Revenge* programme on the 30th of January 1995. Yes, five years on they are still saying I'm a guilty man.

What a terrible Christmas present for Lee; there within that write-up was his mother cuddled by Roy Brown. Inset was a photograph of me underneath which it said, *George Armstrong jailed after a Frenzy of Hate.* The only hate I can find is the hate Carol must have for me, and God only knows why. But she is intent on keeping her campaign of hatred going.

The season of good will to all men passed but I felt no happiness that cold December. In my mind, I lived the other Christmases that had passed. I thought of the times we had spent in the *Prince of Wales* Hotel on Lord Street, Southport. Those marvellous Christmas day lunches Carol and I had spent with Lee and Jonathan. I had many hours to pass, many tears to wipe away.

With New Year on the doorstep, I did my best to feel optimistic. No one wanted my story; I was an old man.

One very hurtful memory of that Christmas is what Carol did with the Christmas cards I had sent to my sons Jonathan and David. The cards I had sent care of Carol's mother. I asked her to pass them on. Apparently Doris rang Carol and told her the cards were there along with some birthday cards. Carol went over to her mother's, opened all the cards, read them, and then threw them on the fire - including one from Lee. I think it was right for Doris to tell me this because it made me realise how very cold and callous she had become towards Lee and me.

Realising that I stood alone, I knew it was vital that I started to take control of my appeal in every possible way. I had to rely on the legal system in all the obvious formal ways. But something told me I also had to act for myself. I felt my legal counsel had let me down in the past. Time and time again I went over the two trials, and each time I could see where important facts had not been brought to light. Mr Red, you will recall, lost vital documents in my first trial. Witnesses were never called. Stones were definitely left unturned. So from then on I made a copy of all my documents.

Doris Grey continued to write to me and one day sent me a very pretty card which had some remarkable information. A portion of that card I will quote; it says:

I knew about all the books and leaflets sent by Terry as I saw them before going into court. They were in Terry and April's writing (The part of the request for them to be sent) also the name was spelt Browne. It was funny but not when someone else has to take the blame.

It turned out Carol had shown her mother these items before going into court. They had been in Roy Brown's brief case. I could hardly believe what I had read on that card. It implied that Carol and Roy also must have known who had sent them. They had deliberately withheld this information in a bid to add this to their phony case.

So now I had gathered more new evidence - evidence that should have been brought to light long ago. Once again I made notes and would ensure my legal people would hear of this.

But now I had a back-up plan. All new evidence regarding the contract threat, the letters, all the information I had obtained was duplicated. When I had made copies, I sent all documents to the court of appeal. No one knew I was doing this - certainly not my legal people who were handling the appeal. I just couldn't leave anything to chance, nor trust anyone to put my case forward. Experience had taught me I had to back it up.

I had been told not to speak in both trials. I still couldn't speak, but I was determined what I wanted to say would be heard. Within those documents was a letter from Doris Grey confirming Terry Lyed had made the contract threat call. This would lead me to make further enquiries into that matter.

It seemed now so many things were starting to come to light and I was to obtain tremendous help from Mr and Mrs Smith.

They had learnt, via one of my sons, that one of the jury members, from my trial, knew of the Armstrong family. This of course should have been looked into at the time. As you are aware, if you know the defendant within a case, you are supposed to inform the court and step down as a jurist. Although this was a small morsel of information, this too was noted and I informed Mr White who would be acting for me at the Appeal Court if and when I was heard.

At one of my visits, I suggested to Mrs Smith that it would be a good idea to pay a visit to this jurist and ask him if it was in fact the contract threat tape that had convinced him and most of the jury that I was in fact guilty. This may sound a little desperate but I had to follow every possible avenue.

Mr and Mrs Smith, ever helpful in my cause, found out where the gentleman lived and went to see him. As it turned out, he was an ex-policeman. The gentleman was cordial with his visitors, and yes, he confirmed it was indeed the contract threat that had helped to convince him and the other jury members that I was guilty of hiring a Hit Man. The man said the tape was played several times in the jury room. So without doubt that tape had weighed heavily against me.

If nothing else, this must have ruffled the feathers of the police force. I say this because strange happenings came about as a result of this visit.

The next day Mrs Smith told me what the ex-jurist had told her. Armed with that information, I wrote to the Chief Constable of

Liverpool, again putting forward the fact that it was obvious the contract threat tape had been instrumental in securing my conviction. As this tape had been joined up with calls I had made in March 1990 to Roy Brown, surely such a ploy had been intended to misdirect the jury. Worse, it was evidence that had been tampered with. The calls I made had been hand-picked for the doctored tape. I start off sounding drunk, then sober, then drunk again. So they were not in any actual order.

The response? Well maybe the ex-jurist informed the police of Mr and Mrs Smiths' visit - he was an ex policeman after all. Or perhaps it was my letter to the Chief Constable citing the injustice I had suffered along with certain vital matters overlooked in the case. Whatever it was, two months later Mr and Mrs Smith had a visit from two plain-clothes detectives who asked why they had visited the ex-jurist. Mrs Smith told them why. The officers said they should not bother this gentleman again, nor make any other moves of that nature. Should they do so they would be arrested and prosecuted. The two officers also insisted they visit Crosby police station and make a statement. When they did eventually go there, they saw an Inspector. This gentleman was very nice to them. He sympathised with them and said he understood that they were only trying to help an innocent man find justice. Nonetheless they had to sign a document stating they would not go near the jurist again. What was more enlightening was what the Inspector said to them. His advice was, "Leave it alone." These words were as good as saying, "Back off."

Thankfully the Smiths continued to assist me in proving my innocence, and thank God they did. They stood by me and Lee and I am eternally grateful.

So why were the police so worried? I had been in prison for over a year. Maybe on reflection Inspector Dorkins could see he had been lazy, and that he had made mistakes. Perhaps. Whatever the reason, Inspector Dorkins had played with a set of marked cards and dealt me a terrible hand of fate. For there is no way round it. That edited contract tape changed my fate.

In Kirkham, life went on and I lived for the day I would leave there for good. My days of liberty were a great comfort to me and I even had the opportunity to go along and see how the Cherryfield Club was progressing.

The Cherryfield was the club in which I had invested two hundred thousand pounds, and which, because of my predicament with the law, I had foolishly handed over to my nephew. The plan, arranged whilst I was on bail, as you may recall, was that he would get the place up and running. He made no financial investment into this venture. His fifty percent interest was given to him. All he had to do was ensure the club would progress and open. He would be in control, the manager. In doing this I gave Gordon Twist a golden opportunity to make a future for himself.

The day I called to see him at the Cherryfield was the same day I had been to see the head at Lee's school. Lee was understandably having a few problems at school; he was so confused with things. His little world had collapsed,and though he had two good people caring for him, he had virtually lost his Mom and Dad. This coupled with the bullying and name calling had disrupted his education. So my visit to his school was very important to me. After the visit to the school, I went on to my club - the club I had once owned but in which I now held only a fifty percent share. Gordon met me, shook my hand and confirmed our agreement was as good as ever. Lil, my ex-wife was with me at that meeting. I felt encouraged, for I was now feeling confident that I would win my appeal. I told him so, and said I would be back there with him. On my return we would forge ahead to even greater success. He smiled and agreed. I had no reason to doubt him - he was my sister's boy and his mother was also involved in the business. Little did I know at the time that I never would figure at all in his plans.

On my release from prison my sister and her son told me to get lost. They had no intention of letting me back into my own business. They even rang the police and said I was threatening them. In doing so they made sure an order was placed so that I could not go near my premises until they had gone bankrupt.

But I'm jumping ahead of myself. This was all to come. For the present, it was back to Kirkham and my confined existence there.

Always an industrious person, it seemed no time before I was promoted to a better position. This next post was in the visiting area. I worked alongside WVS ladies who served tea and refreshments. This was a Number One position. I handled money - about six hundred pounds a week - from the sales of goods there. I was trusted, and needed to be as I will explain later. But now let me tell you about my unannounced visitors. Like Mr and Mrs Smiths' visitors, they came in a twosome.

One day I was working away in the visiting office when I was told two officers had come to see me. The men were in plain clothes and I wondered what this was all about. I was asked to join them in the visiting area, which I did. They asked me to sit down and tea was arranged for us.

They began to discuss my case. At the back of my mind, I thought this was all to do with my appeal. But as the conversation moved along, I realised that this was not so. The officers were saying that it was not the fault of the police that I had been found guilty; the blame, they said, lay with the prosecution. I shook my head, and disagreed. I told them that the prosecution could only present what the police put before them and it is the police who, in putting their case together, compile all the evidence to prove their prisoner guilty. I pointed out there had been no such evidence, only the contract threat tape. The officers tried hard to convince me that any blame or grievance I had lay at the door of the prosecution. Then unbelievably one of them brought out a document and casually asked, "Will you sign this George?"

"What's that?" I asked.

I took it from the officer and read it through. The document was in the form of a letter explaining that I had no complaint against police as to their handling of my case. I couldn't believe this. I shook my head and gave it back to them at the same time refusing to sign such a document.

When they asked why, I told them that I did have a complaint about the police, as they were to blame for my wrongful imprisonment. Once again they said I had got it all wrong, that it was not the police who were at fault, that it had been the prosecution. I stood my ground, and said no. What more could they do to me now? I was in prison. I had lost my good name, my home, my business, the company of Lee. I couldn't be hurt anymore.

The officers asked once more, "Are you going to sign this?"

"No" I replied.

They put the letter away and looked a little put out. Within no time at all they decided they had to go. I was very angry about this incident, but oddly, in doing this, the police shot themselves in the foot. If they were blameless why ask me to sign to the fact?

After that visit I wrote a letter to my legal people dealing with the appeal telling them what had transpired. I also sent a copy to the Lord Chief Justice Taylor at the Appeal Court in London, again without telling my counsel I had done so. It was a sorry turn of events. The police blamed the prosecution; the prosecution, the police. I wanted it on record.

I continued with my job in the visitors' department, which in itself may sound an easy post, but I can assure you it wasn't. Apart from serving tea, biscuits, chocolates, etc you had to work with other inmates. Some stole the goods, others were difficult. I had one occasion when I had to work alongside a child sex offender. At first I wasn't aware of that fact but when I did find out, we had a dispute about it. I didn't want to be near him. Thankfully he was moved.

From other prisoners I was constantly being threatened with assault and verbal abuse was frequent. The reason for both was this. I refused to assist the inmates with their traffic in drugs. The visiting department was used in this manner by prisoners and visitors, but I refused to be a part of it. I risked getting hurt badly for not helping. The threats were very real and I can tell you it was frightening at times.

The way they worked this smuggling was very simple. When visits were concluded, the visitors would leave empty crisp packets, empty bottles, cartons and the like which would then be cleared away. One of my jobs was to tidy up the mess. What inmates wanted me to do was pick up these empty chocolate boxes, cartons, crisp packets that had been left by girlfriends or other visitors. Inside the debris would be drugs or money.

There was no way I would get involved in this at all. I was trusted and I had respect for my position. Regardless of the threats I had to hang on in there. I was awaiting my appeal, and I had to keep strong. If I had weakened, done anything wrong in any shape or form, I would have been sent out to a lock up jail. That I feared more than any threat. Sometimes however they did get to you, like the time I got back to my cell, only to find someone had paid a visit and wrecked it. The visitor had ripped all the photographs of my family off the wall, torn them up and thrown them on the floor. I was so upset with this. The threats also reached out of prison, and they said they would get my family, and that they knew all about the Bingo places. They said they would have the businesses and their homes broken into. These were threats from professional criminals, men dealing in drugs and other serious crimes. I knew they were not idle threats. What is frightening is their power even when locked up.

Amidst all this horror I pursued my quest for freedom. Mrs Smith had helped me get a private investigator who would attempt to obtain a recording of Terry Lyed's voice.

The idea behind this was that with a copy of his voice we could have it compared with the Hit Man threat tape. If we could prove the two voices were one and the same, then at least one mystery would be solved, and the Hit man theory blown away or pursued with someone else.

The investigator, with the help of a microphone, concealed in a brief case managed to get a voice sample which he passed on to Mrs

Smith who sent it along with a copy of the prosecution's Hit man Threat tape to a voice expert in Leeds. Sadly, the expert was not able to do the job as there were not enough vowels on the tape, to make satisfactory comparisons. This expert by the way also did work for the police, and I couldn't help but wonder if that was the real reason he backed off. Either way the tapes were returned and once again my way was blocked. Many stumbling blocks would be set before me in my endeavour to prove my innocence. I had to roll them aside one by one. I thank God for all those who have assisted me in this long journey. Family, friends. Even strangers. I have found truth is a rope many will hold onto, and their strength has helped me constantly bounce back.

Whilst in Kirkham, I became friendly with a man by the name of Jack Parker from Fleetwood. Jack who was only there for a short time was no criminal; he was inside for a misdemeanour regarding his business. We got on quite well. I had told him about the problem of having the taped voices compared officially. He sympathised with my position and said when he was released he would try and help.

Jack left, and I looked forward to hearing from him with the name and address of the voice specialist we had talked of.

For me also things were about to change. Strangely I lost my position in the visiting department and was put on gardening duties. This being a much more demanding role for a man of my years. But maybe there was more to this than I realized. Perhaps it was by way of a punishment for not signing that disclaimer letter - the one saying I had no complaint against the police.

One day when I was sitting in the library, two prison officers I knew came up to me. I had been there seventeen months, and got on with most of the officers, and with these two I was quite friendly and on first name terms. Well, it was really one way terms - they called me George but I always called them 'sir' as is the norm. They both approached me and I noted a rather tight look on both their faces. Then one said to me:

"Come with us George."

"Where to?" I asked.

The officer looked at the other one, then at me. "Across to your cell. You're being shipped out".

I said: "You're joking."

But as I said it, my heart sank. Any kind of move - unless it was freedom - struck horror in me. There couldn't be anywhere as open as Kirkham. Where the hell was I going? We went over to my cell, I got my bits together and then the officers proceeded to go all through my things. They searched through my mail, my documents, everything. When they had finished, they told me why. The Governor had sent them on this search because the police had informed him that I had been demanding money with menaces. I stood there gob-smacked. What the hell was going on? This was too ridiculous for words. I didn't have to demand money from anybody. The officer said nothing, and once again checked through my belongings. As they did so I took the photographs of my children from the wall and gathered little mementos of a past life. Once collected my things were put in a black bag and I was escorted to a cell in Kirkham and locked up. Not long after that a taxi arrived, and I was put in it handcuffed to the two officers. The car drove towards the main gate. I was too shocked to do or say anything. What could I do? I had long ago learned that once the system has you, you are helpless in its mighty hands. All I had was the hope that the pen was mightier than the sword and that one day that pen would cut me free. For now I sat there with these two officers. I think they were as shocked as I was. As we approached the main gate, there stood a certain senior officer - a particularly nasty piece of work. No one liked him, not even the other officers. The car stopped, the man bent down indicating to the officer to open the car window. The senior officer called to me,

"Armstrong, you're going where you belong."

I looked back and said, "How do you mean?"

The officer half smiled and said,

"You're going to a lock-up prison where you belong."

The two officers with me simply sat there saying nothing. They couldn't. Once on the motorway the officers told me I was being taken to Lancaster Jail. In case you don't know, the Jail is the castle in the centre of the city. This is a long term prison, a place that houses life-serving prisoners. Men convicted of violent crime and murder. A secure prison in fact. As they talked, the officers conveyed their sympathy for me being moved. I tried to ask them what it was all about, but they told me they could not discuss it. All they could say is that rumour has it you have been demanding money with menaces from somebody outside.

When I had time to think it out, I felt this was all down to the police. I was being sent to Lancaster because I had not signed that disclaimer letter. I wouldn't let them off the hook and so now they would make sure I was nicely locked up. It was their way of getting back at me.

Arriving at Lancaster I looked around at the cold forbidding walls. From a courtyard I was taken up to reception, from where I was left in a small room, a kind of a waiting room. Whilst in there, a prisoner came and talked with me. He told me he was a lifer, and that Lancaster was a horrible place. I nodded. I had already sensed that. Next I was told to shower again and then was issued with Lancaster prison clothing. It was awful, like going back to the hell of Walton. I dressed in the long-term prison uniform, pulled on the prison boots, as usual too large for me. At Kirkham I had worn my own shoes, and this minor loss was so important. My heart sank as my feet disappeared into those hard boots. Once dressed, I was taken to a wing and pushed into a cell with a lifer. I broke down. I could not believe that this hell could be my fate.

I had been moved without any warning, not even allowed to inform any of my family that I had been moved. I knew when I did tell them they would be worried and upset. Poor Lee again suffering the worst of all.

Next day I made an appointment to see the Governor. I wanted to know exactly why I had been sent there. I also spoke to the senior officer who said he would get me a job with the cleaners, washing trays. But in the meantime I had to see the Deputy Governor.

I was taken to see him with another officer to whom I had been handcuffed. The Deputy informed me once again, only now officially, that yes, I had been moved there because I had been demanding money with menaces from people in the Liverpoool area. The police had passed on this information to them. I said this was ridiculous, that it was all a pack of lies. I had been at Kirkham over a year and if there had ever been any trouble, I would have been moved before. The Deputy said nothing. He was of course unaware of the cloak and dagger work that had stalked my time in prison.

If I had been out of prison demanding money with menaces as the police had claimed, this would have been a criminal offence. The Kray brothers in their heyday had employed this rather distasteful method, alongside murder and other heinous crimes. They had been sent to prison for it. Now, the police had put me in a bracket with the likes of people like that.

****

184

CHAPTER THIRTEEN
FLIGHT OF FANCY

LANCASTER Prison was a depressing place. There were sad cases too, like a young boy I came to know. The boy, a young man really, was in there serving a life sentence. He had apparently committed a murder in the south somewhere. Whilst I do not condone what he did in any way, I found I could not turn my back on the lad.

Maybe it was because I was so much older that he latched on to me. I suppose I was a bit of a father figure to him. We came to know one another purely by circumstance.

Due to my age, me being a lot older than most prisoners there, I had been placed on the ground floor. The cell in fact faced the serving department where food was given out. Prisoners queued outside this area, and that is how I came to know him. His name? Well, let's call him Ben. Ben used to wait until the other prisoners had gone, and then he would turn up. He started to call to me, and then came over a couple of times to my cell. We got chatting and I told him I was waiting for my appeal. He said he was waiting for his to come up too. This seemed to establish a common interest, and besides I felt sorry for him. He used to ask me questions and brought some of his documents to me a couple of times. Ben had been in prison eight or nine years. He'd been moved many times and wherever he was placed he'd been beaten up. Ben was a real victim himself. He appeared vague about things, and in my opinion the lad was simple and certainly not equipped to cope with prison life, which regardless of all you hear, is hard. Ben certainly wasn't hard, but he had been given a hard time by a system that didn't know how and where to place him. He wanted to be moved back down south so he could have his father visit him, but so far that little dream had not come true. I really only knew what Ben told me so I can't make too much judgement.

What was tragic about this situation was that Ben had been waiting for his appeal all those years. As I have said earlier, if you are waiting for an appeal, you surely should not have to mix with cruel and vicious men, prisoners who took great pleasure in tormenting weaker or lesser mortals, men who enjoyed inflicting pain, men who would abuse their fellow man just for the kick of it, sexual or otherwise, killers who were never remorseful and had no deterrent that would stop them from killing again, men who managed to acquire drugs and at their highest edge of feeling would prefer murder and mayhem to any other activity. These evil people exist and whilst do-gooders make excuses for them, the fact is those mortals are just evil through and through. These are the men I lived with, these are the men Ben lived with too. I think Ben took strength in the fact I was so engrossed in my appeal. He couldn't help himself the way I had done even though his father was doing his best from the outside. Ben was tormented in Lancaster, and he wanted to be moved. One night someone had done something to the lock on his cell door, and consequently he had to spend the night in another cell. This had disturbed him greatly.

One evening Ben came into my cell and sat on my bed. I asked him what he was going to do that evening. Was he going to the library? He shook his head,

"No, I'm going to watch television," he replied.

I noticed he was wearing new trainers. Though Ben was about twenty six, he seemed a lot younger than his years. I made a comment saying how nice the trainers were and his face lit up like that of a little boy. His swung his legs pleased with himself. He said his Dad had just sent them that day, and that his Dad had said his appeal hearing was only a few days away. I was pleased for him.

Half an hour later that boy was dead. He went up to his cell, and two or three prisoners attacked him there. They lifted him up bodily and smashed his head on the sink. Apparently they had nearly cut his head off, and not content with that, had smashed all the bones in his body. They left this horror on the landing for the officers to deal with.

I knew nothing of this until later. The first thing we all heard were the bells and we were sent back to our cells. Once inside I peered out of my window, and there down the stairs went the officers carrying a body bag. I still had no idea who it was.

When I heard it was Ben who had been murdered, I broke down. This place was hell - there was no other word for it. How could anyone do this vile cruel thing? What kind of vermin were eating and sleeping amongst us. Here we all were locked up together with them, the faceless masks of human flesh were all you saw. You never knew what lay behind those eyes that met with yours. What made things even more frightening was the fact the prison officers themselves seemed powerless to stop such acts. I was devastated. I felt unbalanced. I was amongst unbalanced men. I started to forget things, and I began to question my own sanity. I was so shaken by this event that it actually pulled me down physically and I became so ill that I ended up in the prison hospital.

It was whilst I was being treated there that I once again had two unannounced visitors. In anticipation, I went up to the visitors department. What a surprise it was! There they were, the same two officers that had visited me in Kirkham. The very same high rank-ing Inspectors. Our meeting was cordial; we exchanged words once again about my case. Once again they asked me to sign the document. A letter, by way of a disclaimer saying that I had no complaint against the police. I shook my head, and told them no. I would not sign. When they accepted I was not going to sign, they got up and left; two very annoyed police officers I can tell you.

To my mind it was all too clear what was going on. I had been sent to Lancaster because I would not sign the disclaimer. They had concocted this lie about me threatening people for money with menaces. Once again the great wheel of injustice had turned, and the police were putting all hands to the wheel to make sure I had a hard time. They had blackened my name and they intended to heap on the agony. So far they had made a very good job of it. From the start, a conspiracy of lies had put me in prison, and those lies were now aimed from a distance and fixed onto me. I was trapped, a sitting target for them.

As always, I made sure my legal people knew of this and under cover I ensured the appeal court knew of this second attempt to obtain my signature to a document I could not honestly sign.

On the plus side, Jack whom I had met in Kirkham, the man who was going to find me a voice analyst, had tracked me down to Lancaster. He came to visit me there and told me that within a few days he would have the gentleman's name and address. Good as his word, a few days later I received a letter from him giving me the name and address of a man prepared to go ahead with this work. On the minus side, what I did not know was the fact that Mr Roy Brown and the firm he worked for, were representatives of the Prison Officers' Association. What then transpired was this.

Someone from Lancaster Jail informed the police as to the content of that particular letter and made sure I would hit problems in trying to prove who that voice belonged to.

Once I had the letter, I rang Mrs Smith and told her I had someone who could now make a comparison between the Contract Threat tape and the voice sample the investigator had obtained. I passed on all the details to her, the man's name and address and she said she would get in touch with him next day.

As always, Mrs Smith did as she said, and she rang him. But there would be bad news for her. The man had already been contacted by the police. They had advised him it would be better if he did not take on this work as their could be a clash of interests. It seems this man also did work for the police. It was clear they were saying once again: "Back off." This time to a professional man they use themselves! What this man did agree to do was talk to a colleague of his who lived in London. He told her he too was an expert in this field and possibly would be able to assist us. He said he would ring him, and then get him to ring her.

It is quite evident this man could see the police were acting oddly in this matter. At the same time he knew he could not tread on their toes. By making sure his colleague rang Mrs Smith he concealed any possible information as to the identity or address of the other voice expert. In other words, he smelt a rat.

Mrs Smith was called by the other gentleman, who lived and worked at a university in the south. The man was a highly qualified individual and I was happy to proceed with my endeavour.

But this was a blatant move by the police in a bid to stop me from getting to the truth. They were embarrassed, as they knew they had much to hide in the matter. Thankfully this particular stumbling block was to be overcome.

The voice analyst in London processed both tape samples and this is what he said.

In summary, the differences were not sufficient to eliminate Mr Lyed as the Hit Man caller. Indeed, taking into consideration the characteristics of the two recordings and evaluating the phonetic and acoustic data, overall. I consider that Mr Lyed made the Hit Man call.

This section of the report from a professor, with qualifications as long as your arm, cannot be ignored, nor disputed. That document is dated the 23rd of the 12th 1992.

The fee for this exercise was £400 and the money was paid by cheque, the person who had helped me in this way being Lillian. Lil, and my son Gary, had financed all the unsuccessful appeals and stood by me stoically. At one turn of events, Mr Red had taken £1,000 from Gary in an attempt to make an appeal on my behalf.

This turned out to be a sham, and the money was lost for good. This should not have happened and I have to question the professionalism in this connection.

Mr Red, as I have said earlier, lost documents that were vital to my case. I also feel he did not present certain evidence to Mr White my barrister. Still I had to deal with these people, and even today I find myself still locked into this circle. There seems no way of stopping the wheel turning.

But let me get back to the 'Contract' tape. I was thrilled to have this evidence. It proved what others had told me. At last I had it in black and white. If I had been guilty, I would hardly have wanted the man flushed out - that is the last thing I would have sought. So surely now the law, the police (well, *some* of the police) would see I was innocent!

On a visit, my barrister had said to me, "George, prove the tape, and we are home and dry."

Well I had done what he had asked - I had proved the identity of the caller. By doing so we ruled out the very basis of my alleged attack.

But then Mr White had not always been so confident. Weeks before I was moved to Lancaster, he had said,

"I can't take this. I think you'd better get somebody else."

I was dismayed at this. Who on earth could I replace him with? The law and the police had served me very badly - such that I felt I could never trust them again.

I was also told by someone that Roy Brown knew every move I made in prison. That was no surprise to me, but what twisted pleasure could he gain by having me tucked away? I had not done him any harm, even at my worst on those phone calls I had made. Like any average person when really angry, I said some regretful things. But the gist was, I was going to finish him in his career.

In February 1993 I was called to the Governor's office. He had good news for me. My appeal date had been set for two weeks ahead! I would be going up to London on the 25th of February! I was overjoyed. I knew I was so close to freedom now. The past months had been absolutely horrendous. I had also spent my third Christmas in prison. I thought the first two had been bad enough but there in Lancaster, such an evil place, I had suffered the most.

Before the appeal I was allowed a day at liberty again. Jack who had put me in touch with the voice specialist graciously offered to come and pick me up. He drove me back to Merseyside, and we went to visit Lil and she gave us a wonderful lunch. We then visited one of the bingo clubs and saw my sons. Then Jack came and met Lee with whom we stayed for about two hours after which Jack drove me back to Lancaster. I had to be back there for five thirty. We arrived there, Jack wished me luck, and I returned to that dark part of my life. But this time hope was very much by my side.

Next morning when I went about one of my jobs there, I felt perhaps life was going to change for me. That morning job involved me getting the trays ready for the prisoners to have their breakfast. In order to do this job, I was allowed out of my cell about fifteen minutes earlier than the other prisoners. I got into a habit whilst on this particular duty of collecting all the bits of bread that had been left. I looked in the bins on the exercise yard, in the hope of finding more stale bread. I would break up the bread, take it out to the exercise yard, stand in the centre and throw the bread around for the many, many pigeons there in Lancaster; it seemed as though there were hundreds of them perched high in the roof areas, the alcoves, anywhere they could. With it being an old castle, there were plenty of vantage points to nest.

I think my white hair was some kind of beacon to them for they would fly down and anticipate the bread being thrown for them. I did this religiously every morning and it was a practice I enjoyed as much as the pigeons.

But ten days before I was due to go on my appeal, I was called to the office of the senior security officer.

He looked formally at me and asked me to sit down. Also present were three other officers who also looked uncomfortable. I braced myself. Bad news was something I had got used to. I dreaded what was to come. The senior officer leaned across the desk, and linked his fingers. My heart started to thud. The officer then went on to tell me that he had received privileged information that I was going to escape from the prison. I must have turned white. I shook my head vigorously.

"This is ridiculous - you're joking," I said. "Escape from here! How can you escape from here?"

I was so worried, and I thought, 'Here we go again; they are trying to put the brakes on my appeal.' I was genuinely concerned.

The officer then shook his head. "I am joking, George. Read this and sign it."

I think I was shaking by now. I took the sheet of paper he handed to me and read it. This is what it said:

Sir,

Information has come to hand that Armstrong 295 is planning an escape attempt.

We believe that on the morning of Tuesday the 16th of Feb '93, he plans to be carried out of prison by a flock of approx. 5000 pigeons which he has been secretly training on the exercise yard over the last 3 months. He has been heard muttering to the flock leaders that he had bread secreted in his underpants for payment.

However on the plus side, we expect Armstrong to be returned by tea-time lock-up, as he has not calculated that they are homing pigeons.

For your attention sir.

I burst out laughing, partly from relief, partly from joy. The officers laughed with me. When we had settled, they all shook my hand and wished me well. The senior officer even slapped me on the back when wishing me well.

That was a very human touch. I had almost forgotten how to laugh. But I think this goes some way to showing you that I had behaved in prison, that I had toed the line. This had been my attitude all through. I treated the officers with respect and they in turn were fine with me. There are always one or two people who never take to you. Perhaps it was one of these individuals who was reporting back to those who wanted to know what I was doing. Even on my last night before going up to London for the appeal, a strange thing happened. Someone pushed an envelope under my door. When I picked it up and opened it there was a photograph of Roy Brown torn out of a prison officer's magazine. Roy Brown being one of their representative solicitors gazed up at me smiling. I looked back at this face, a face that had watched me in the dock, a face that had lied. I then pushed the face back in the envelope. The person who did this must have been the man who had been asked to watch me. Probably it was he who had informed the police that I was contacting a voice analyst. But he wouldn't have acted alone - there must have been someone directing him.

So the day arrived for me to travel up to London for my appeal. I was very excited. I had packed all my stuff, and I was so confident I would not be coming back I gave away my radio and also some other little bits and pieces.

I was first taken to reception where there were two other prisoners. We were handcuffed together and then taken out to the transport van. The three officers who would escort us then climbed in the van and we set off.

It was going to be a long journey, we would be handcuffed all the way, but I didn't care anymore. I had this wonderful feeling that I would soon be a free man again.

On the way down we stopped at a prison in Cannock near Birmingham. This was by way of a break for the officers and us. Inside the prison the officers went to their own quarters, whilst we were placed in cells and given a meal. We stayed there over an hour, and it was nice to have that time to wash and freshen up. Then once again we made our way to London. The officers were smashing lads, and we all had a laugh with them, which helped to relieve any tension. The other two prisoners were going on their appeals too, and so we were all a little nervous and excited all at the same time.

We arrived in London about five thirty as dusk was falling. We were heading for Brixham prison where we would be staying until our appeal hearing. On arrival there, we were placed in cells. Mine was not very clean, and a bucket which had not been emptied for some time stood in a corner. It turned my stomach - I could never adjust to this indignity. Brixham is a very old building, and the bucket was the toilet facility. A very archaic and unhygenic method. But still I told myself I would soon be saying goodbye to all this.

Next morning we were taken down to reception, where we learned that the other two prisoners would be going for their appeal on a different day. So I would be going to court on my own that particular morning. Two of the officers who had escorted me from Lancaster took me down to the van. It was a little easier being with the same officers, as we had got to know each other a little, though this was still all very formal.

As we drove through London towards the High Courts of the Old Bailey, I started to feel shaky. This was so important to me. Yes I was confident it would all be okay, but two years of being locked away had instilled a hidden fear in me. The truth had let me down once before, and all I had now was that same truth. Yes, I now had gathered new evidence, but would it be brought to light? The truth had been hidden before. Would it get a chance to show its strength? My heart missed a beat, and I felt my chest tightening. Please God, I prayed, let justice be done for the sake of my son Lee. He needs me. Oh yes, I prayed.

The date was February the 25th 1993, but to me it was so much more than a number in a month. That day could change my whole life for the better or it could sentence me to death. For in my heart I knew that if I had to go back to Lancaster I was sure to die there.

Once at the Old Bailey, I was taken to the cells below. It was about eight fifteen in the morning, and the courts would not start till ten. So I had more time again to go over those two harrowing years locked away for a crime I did not commit. Now the confidence and elation hid themselves in the corner of my mind. I was frightened for this was so important to me. Had I done all in my power to make sure the appeal Judges had the facts at hand? Would my counsel speak up for me? I sat there torturing myself. I went over what other prisoners had told me about their appeals, - appeals that had failed. I was aware I would not be able to speak at all; this was not allowed. So I knew it was vital that my counsel put over all those items of new evidence.

Eventually Mr White came down with Mr Red. After obvious courtesies they proceeded to tell me what points they were going to put forward for my appeal case. What I heard was not what I was hoping for. I had written to Mr White and Mr Red asking them to ensure Doris Grey would be there to confirm her statement as to who the voice was on the contract threat. I also had requested that the voice analyst be present to give his professional opinion on the voice comparisons. Mr White and Mr Red informed me they were not there, and they would not be necessary.

My heart sank. I swallowed. Why hadn't they made sure these people were there - they were vital to my new evidence. 'Here we go again' I thought. In my first two trials, witnesses had not been called on my behalf. Why I will never know. They were willing to come forward, but my legal people, the very same Mr White and Mr Red, had not called them. As they talked, my mind wondered. Why hadn't they called those witnesses in my first two trials? Like the doctor who could have confirmed Carol had threatened to commit suicide, how I had the welfare people involved because of the way she was leaving the children, how Mrs Kemp could have confirmed that Carol had confided in her about the many men in her life. My young beautiful wife was aware of her effect on men. She used them as a tool to get what she wanted. Then she dropped them for the fools they had been. I was her biggest fool, but I won't be her last fool. Roy Brown must have known Carol was in bed with another man the night before he was attacked. A man perhaps with more reason to hate him than I had. Still the court was not allowed to know this at my two trials. How could this have happened? Now my counsel once again were expecting me to trust them.

They went on and I half listened - they were telling me the same old story. My only hope now was that the information I had sent direct to the court, unbeknown to my counsel, would be taken into consideration.

The meeting over, they left to prepare for the court, and I was left to wait in my cell. Eventually, I heard keys being turned in my lock and my name being called. The officers handcuffed me and took me up to the High Court. My heart pounded and I was really afraid. This meant everything to me. The officer told me to sit on a bench outside one of the courts where my case was to be heard. It was Court Number One.

The officers sitting with me advised me not to say anything whilst the case was in process. Soon a gentleman came from the court and indicated for me to go in. The two officers stood up and we went inside. I felt so small in this very big court room. I was escorted up to a little box situated high up in the court. I looked up to my left and there sat the three distinguished Judges. The wigs and gowns every bit as regal and fine as this great room I had been taken to. My eyes glanced at each Judge, their purple robes and sashes indicating their seniority and standing. I was told to sit down. At some distance below us were seated the legal people involved with my case. Mr White and Mr Red were there, and so was Mr Black who had acted for the prosecution. I looked to the back where witnesses, and press were allowed to sit. The benches were empty. I could however see a number of police officers amongst whom sat Inspector Dorkins, the man who, more than any-one, had engineered my conviction. My head faltered and hung down. 'Oh God, please help me' was running through my mind. I knew I had to be silent; this was going to be the quietest fight of my life. Would the lies be K.O 'd?

Would the truth fight back? I had been nearly two and a half years in training. I hoped to God I would get a good clean fight.

Seconds out. The legal people below started to give blow by blow accounts. The prosecution, for their case; the defence, for theirs. High above them I listened as did the learned Judges. After half an hour I started to panic inside. What I was hearing was old news. This was the very stuff that had put me away. I wanted to scream out, "No, no - that isn't right." I so much wanted to speak for myself, it was agonising. The Judges looked solemn and fixed as they listened. What on earth would they make of all this? Had they, I wondered, read what I had sent to the court. I looked, listened and waited. When the legal people below had concluded, there was a pause whilst they settled.

I looked up at the Lord Chief Justices and as I did the Judge in the middle - this being Justice Steyn - spoke. In a slow deliberate voice, he said:

"Mr White, will you kindly tell me about Tenerife?"

This question directed at my defence counsel pricked up my ears. I looked down to Mr White who appeared visibly shaken. He looked over to Mr Black for the prosecution who also looked very taken aback. They were both shocked - there was no doubt about it. Suddenly I felt the strength coming back to me; the truth had just landed an upper cut - right on the spot it went. They must have been knocked for six. So my ploy had worked - the copy documents I had sent had reached these three good Judges.

"Tell me about Tenerife."

What a question! This of course referred to the time Carol had said she was going to the shops, and that she would be back in a few minutes. After several hours had passed and I had tried to trace her via friends, I reported her missing to the police.

The police being concerned asked for her passport and took it with them. Later, very much later, it would be revealed that Carol had spent several days in Tenerife with Roy Brown. He had said it was coincidence that they were both there at the same time. This coincidental get together had been in September 1989. At my trials they had sworn on oath that they had not started their affair until January 1990. In a word both had perjured themselves and proved how well they could lie and to what lengths they would go to cover their lies.

I looked down anxiously as both counsels looked under their desks for their files. My counsel had no plan to bring this to the notice of the appeal Judges. But why? It was vital in showing the lack of credibility and honesty in all that they said about me. I could only think that the legal profession was trying to protect one of their own. Embarrassed Mr White shuffled around for the relevant paperwork.

Eventually, it was brought to hand and Mr White asked if he might speak. Lord Justice Steyn indicated that he could. Mr White then went on to read out the incident regarding Tenerife. I looked at the stern face of Justice Steyn. On one side of him was Mr Justice Garland; on the other, Mr Justice Rougier. All paid great attention to what was being said.

When Mr White had finished, Justice Steyn made one comment that stuck in my mind. He said,

"Would that not indicate Mr Brown was telling lies?"

My heart leapt for joy. My prayers were being answered; the truth was starting to come out at last. The long faces of the legal people below grew longer as they realized the Judges were questioning the tactics of both counsels. I could see my case was finally having a fair hearing.

"I'm coming home to Lee," I thought. "I'm coming home to Lee."

****

198

CHAPTER FOURTEEN
IN MY LIVERPOOL HOME

I N SUMMING up, Lord Justice Steyn made many points - for example:

"From now until 12th July 1990 when the last alleged threat was made, the prosecution case about threats is entirely dependent on the evidence of Mr Brown, the solicitor. That was a somewhat fragile basis for the prosecution case on that aspect. In due course the judge made strong comments about Mr Brown's credibility and his exaggerations. Undoubtedly he minimised his own role and his relationship. In any event on Mr Brown's evidence, the last telephone call making a threat was made on 12th July 1990.

The attack on Mr Brown took place on 17th August 1990. A Stanley knife was used. The assailant viciously attacked him and he was lucky to survive. Mr Brown was unable to recognise the assailant. It has to be said that he subsequently wrongly identified somebody else as being the assailant.

Pausing there and taking stock of the prosecution case, the position is that Carol Armstrong could contribute very little to the prosecution case. She was tendered for cross-examination. She was not put forward as a credible witness because in the middle of the trial she had phoned the appellant about his continued plea of not guilty and tried to put pressure on him and then lied about that. As far as Mr Brown is concerned I have already explained how the judge dealt with his credibility."

These words were like honey to my ears. These three wise Judges were saying that they also did not believe Carol nor Roy Brown.

Lord Justice Steyn then said:

"The gap between the attack and the threat, if one is to believe Mr Brown, was about one month. If Mr Brown's evidence is not regarded as reliable, then the gap is of the order of about five months. That is how the prosecution case stood."

The Judge went on to say:

"The appellant testified at his trial. He denied that he had anything to do with the attack on Mr Brown. The gist of his evidence was that all he had in mind was that Mr Brown deserved a biff on the nose. He made assertions during his oral evidence about the fact that his wife had continued to have affairs with other men, the suggestion being that that supplied a motive for somebody else to attack Mr Brown."

Further the Lord Justice said:

"We turn now to another matter and it is an aspect of the case which does not appear in the grounds of appeal. It occurred, however, to the court that it was a matter which requires debate. Attention was drawn to both counsels earlier today to this aspect and when the case was later called we have had the benefit of argument on it. The matter which causes us concern is the following. The prosecution case established a motive on the part of the defendant to attack Brown. It also established repeated threats of violence over a lengthy period. If the defendant was involved, it follows that he persuaded somebody else to commit the attack. There was no evidence showing planning of the attack by the defendant. It was not a particularly strong prosecution case, but central to the prosecution case was the need to show that there was a conspiracy between two persons to attack Brown. If there was such a conspiracy the prosecution was able to say with some force that the defendant must have been party to the conspiracy. If such a conspiracy was not established, the defendant was undoubtedly not guilty. Needless to say the defence argued that there was a reasonable doubt as to whether there was such a conspiracy. In particular the defence argued that the reasonable possibility could not be excluded that the attack was undertaken by somebody who was taking the appellant's side in the matrimonial dispute but without his knowledge, or alternatively by a jealous boyfriend of Mrs Armstrong."

In closing the Judge said:

"It is also not to be forgotten that this was a retrial. We mention this only as being some of the material relevant to show that this was a far from straightforward case. It is often difficult to say on which side of the lie a judge's comment on an issue of fact falls. Here the particular issue of fact was the central point in the case and it seems to this court that the judge went further than was warranted, while the rest of the summing-up was entirely fair and balanced, the effect of the earlier comments would have, in our judgment, lingered on. Effectively the judge's comments undermined the prospect that the jury might consider that it was not proved beyond reasonable doubt that there was a contract to attack Mr. Brown. The judge was certainly entitled to take the view that the defence was an implausible one, but no matter how implausible a defence may seem to a judge a defendant is in our adversarial system always entitled to have that issue of fact fairly considered by the jury. In these circumstances we have come to the conclusion that the jury was misdirected on a central issue of fact. In view of that misdirection we have concluded the conviction was not safe and satisfactory and for that reason we have, before a short adjournment allowed the appeal and quashed the conviction".

As the Lord Justice moved forward with his words, I could see he was going to tell me I had won my appeal. My heart started to pound. I felt like I was running up a hill. I felt so exhilarated. My face must have glowed with pleasure, and I could feel tears of joy and sadness welling in my eyes. My emotions were awash. There had been times at this hearing when all hope kept slipping away from me. I felt sure the documents, the information and evidence I had sent to the court of appeal had been ignored. I sat there sure none of these learned men had heard my side of the story. But I was wrong; they had taken the time. I was so thankful to Justice Taylor, Lord Justice Steyn, Mr Justice Garland and Mr Justice Rougier. They had allowed the truth to come off the ropes. Now the truth and I had to fight on for justice.

I looked down at the barristers; both looked drawn and shocked at the outcome. I then looked at the Judges. I wasn't supposed to speak but I had to.

I said, "I thank you gentlemen, thank you very much indeed."

The officers with me tugged at my coat indicating I shouldn't have spoken. The three eminent men looked towards me. They did not respond, but Lord Justice Steyn offered a guarded smile. A smile worth so much to me. At last I had found justice. I had lost all faith in the law, but here now I had been reassured. One truth can beat a million lies. One truth that many had believed in. One by one they had come to help me because they knew the value of the truth.

The officers took me from the court room. patted me on the back and congratulated me. They told me they knew I would be released. Laughing, joking, we then went down to the waiting room. I was told to sit down and I was given a cup of tea. I was used to being told what to do, and so I obeyed and sat down. My mind really couldn't take it all in. All that I had worked for, all that I had fought for had happened. I felt so upset by it all - elation, panic, joy. I felt them all. I also suddenly felt weak and much older. What now? Where the hell was I going from here? How could I face the world? Part of me wanted to run away and hide, run away and die some- where. If it had not been for my children, it would have been easy to do that. But they deserved more from me. My first family had been a rock, several rocks. The strongest Lil. I didn't deserve such a family, but I thank God for them.

Then there was Lee who could never really be close to his step brothers and sisters. How could he? His mother was the cause of all that had gone wrong for the Armstrongs. No, Lee needed me more than anyone on earth now. I trembled as the cup touched my lips. I felt broken and I was afraid of facing life again. I really did not know how and where to begin.

After a little while I was taken to a reception area, and I was asked a few questions about my imprisonment, also about my health and whether I needed to see a doctor. I shook my head. I was fine, I told them. 'Fine'. It's odd how we make these courteous remarks at the most devastating times. Then they asked me to sign documents - my release papers! My hand shook as I wrote. My emotions so near the surface, but I held on to what little self esteem I had left. Next they asked me to sign for the forty one pounds I was entitled to. I signed and took the cash. Then came a document for a railway ticket, a ticket that would be taking me back to Liverpool. The officers shook my hand, as did the gentleman involved in the paperwork. I was then given a plastic bag with H.M. PRISON SERVICE boldly printed on it. I stuffed all my bits and pieces into it. In went papers and notes regarding my case. Items I had carried from prison to prison. Family photos little mementos. All were tatty now, but these precious bits had helped me to hang on when all seemed hopeless. As they opened the door with a key, I stepped forward and walked to freedom.

I was in the high courts, walking along the long passage ways. All around there was the buzz of people. Barristers with wigs, people talking to court officials. Some sitting, waiting. It was just wonderful to be able to move amongst them. Like a ghost I drifted through. This great old building had seen all life pass by. Now in the corner of its eye it could see me leaving. I hoped it smiled the way Lord Justice Steyn had smiled.

I glanced back once more at those dressed in wigs and gowns. It was all so old fashioned but somehow just perfect. But then I had found justice there.

I walked towards the main entrance and could see a security guard on duty. As I approached him he looked at my plastic bag, he smiled and said,

"You're out?"

I nodded and said, "Yes."

He said, "Congratulations. Off you go." I walked outside the courts and stood there for a moment. I was still very shaken by all that had happened. Cars passed by, some of them taxis, and I waved one down. It stopped, and the driver asked where I was going.

"Euston station, please," I said.

The taxi driver nodded and told me to get in. I sat there watching people on pavements. I opened the window for some air. I found myself constantly near to tears. I was free but somehow lost. I suddenly felt very alone. The taxi driver then asked me if I had just come out, and I told him yes. He had seen the bag with H.M. PRISONS on it. So there was no use trying to hide the fact. I told him I had been in prison, that I had been wrongly convicted, and that I had just been released on appeal. He listened and seemed a nice friendly chap. Then after a few minutes, he said.

"Hang on a minute."

He pulled up by some shops, climbed out, and went into one of the shops. I watched him, puzzled as to what he was doing. He came out of the shop and back to the taxi. He opened the door and gave me a large brown plastic bag.

"Here, put that bag in here then nobody will know."

I did as he said and thanked him very much. He drove me on to Euston station. We talked on the way and he was a really nice chap and I felt a little better for his company. When we arrived at the station, I climbed out and asked him how much I owed him.

"Nothing," he replied.

I shook my head and said, "No, how much is the fare please?"

The taxi driver shook his head. "Nothing, that's free. That's on me. Off you go."

I stood my ground, but he wouldn't have it. He'd taken the time to get me that plastic bag, he'd driven me to the station and wanted nothing for his trouble. I shook his hand, thanked him so much and he drove away. What a wonderful man. Whoever you are I hope your kindness to others is returned a hundredfold.

I stood there, watched him go, and made my way to check the Liverpool platform. As I walked along, my mind went back to the appeal. I recalled the look on the barristers' faces when Lord Justice Steyn said to my defence counsel,

"Tell me about Tenerife."

Thank God he had said that for if it had been left to my counsel, I feel sure I would not have won the appeal. As my mind went back to that moment, I saw Mr Red walking into the station. I felt he intended avoiding me, but we were too close.

Our eyes met, and he said, "Hello George. Nice to get released isn't it? If you consider suing the police, will you contact me on Monday?"

I nodded. I was too drained to be thinking clearly. My energy had been given to the months that had passed. Today had been a crescendo, and I was numb.

"Okay, I'll give you a ring," I replied.

Mr Red smiled and walked away. I went and sat down and looked ahead. I was disgusted with him and Mr White. In the court they had ignored me. They were obviously angered by the fact I had sent back up material to the Court of Appeal. But then if they had done as I asked in the first place, my defence case would have been much stronger in those two costly trials. I had made them look silly perhaps. One thing was clear: in the court they had cold-shouldered me. Not one of them bothered to come and congratulate me on my success. They had abandoned me. Why hadn't they come down to see me? The officers, the court staff, all had wished me well. The very people who were supposed to be representing me

205

had been conspicuous by their absence. I sat there listening to train announcements, watching people hurrying about their business. I had to question the attitude of those legal people who were so interlocked with solicitors. Had they been incompetent with my case or had they deliberately been protecting one of their own? Whatever the answer, because of them and the police, I was a ruined man.

I stood up and made my way to a phone box and rang Mrs Smith to tell her I was free. She was thrilled to bits, and she said she would tell Lee when she picked him up from school. She went on to tell me to go and get a cup of tea and catch the train home.

"Lee will be waiting for you here," she said.

Once on the train, my mind travelled back over the years. I thought about my first family, the girls and boys who now had families of their own. I thought about Lil, the hurt and shame I must have caused her. I lowered my head in shame, my heart saddened by self-reproach. Lil who had been so loyal to me even aiding me financially over these two and half years in prison. I thought of Lee, a boy all alone in the world. All he had was his Dad, now an old man. How was I going to provide for this growing teenager? How could he ever understand that life was not going to be easy for us? I was almost a pensioner, and his life hadn't even started yet. Then I thought of David and Jonathan - sons that I had lost, and I felt that loss deeply. Taking them from me, not letting them see either me or their brother Lee was the unkindest cut of all. Little was I to realise that punishment was to be ongoing.

I recalled my old Mecca days, my business training ground. I thought about the Princes Bingo club, my first business venture. The memories became jumbled as thoughts of Carol came into view. There had been plenty of good times we had shared, but now the memories had soured. Now I could only see her with Roy Brown. The two of them sitting there in the court room, their eyes piercing, their aim to have me put away. I pushed those thoughts away. I didn't want to dwell on that particular part of my life. I had relived it daily for over two years. I was out now, and I had a lot to do in what could be a very short space of time.

I reached for the plastic bag I had pushed under my seat. I pulled out some bits of paper and a pen and started to make notes. I had to draw up a plan of action to go forward. I had nowhere to live. I would probably have to stay in a hotel until I got sorted. I made a note to ring my family on arrival in Liverpool. I thought if I got stuck, maybe one of them would put me up for a few days until I found somewhere to live. I didn't want to have to do this; I hated the thought of imposing on them. I am old fashioned, and I believe in the saying, 'As you make your bed, so you must lie in it.' But I was at rock bottom, and had to swallow what little pride I had left. As I scribbled away I sipped the cup of tea I had obtained from the tea bar close by. Already I had broken into my forty one pound release money. I gazed out at fields, I heard the laughter of passengers nearby and started to acclimatize myself to my new freedom. I thought about this book too and I scribbled notes that I felt would be useful. I also thought about the police, and in particular that Inspector who was always so sure he had arrested the right man. He had been so smug, so sure of himself, but he had always been wrong. What I wonder was he going to make of things now? Here I was on my way back - I had proved him wrong. I was also going to sue the police for all that I had lost materially. My good name, the years, the indignity, the heartbreak which could never be compensated for. But I was damn sure they would pay in money for what they had done to me, my family, Lee and the little brothers he had lost touch with.

As the train drew into Liverpool's Lime Street station, I stood by the door ready to get off. Over the years I had had many, many train journeys, but this one was the strangest journey I had ever taken. The train had pulled me all the way from London, it had rushed, slowed down, and stood still a little while. A little like a life story of its own. We rush, slow down, stand and wait. I felt I had travelled a far greater distance on that train. In my mind, I certainly had. I had reflected over sixty years of my life.

I opened the door of the train and stepped down. I clutched my brown plastic bag and walked along towards the entrance. My head hung a little, perhaps in sympathy with the suit that hung limply on my back. I looked up, my half-closed eyes widening with pleasure. Standing there, a short distance away were my family. Their faces half smiles and tears. My first wife Lil, my sons, my daughters. The whole family were there to greet me. They ran to me, kissed me, hugged me. I was so overcome I broke down and cried. We all walked towards the entrance. Outside the station I was surprised to see several press men waiting for me. The photographers moved forward, but my son Lawrence put his arms in front of me, shielding me from them. My other son Mark put his arm round me and pulled me away. The press shouted to us, asking questions.

My sons called, "Ignore them Dad. Ignore them."

My son Lawrence insisted they stopped trying to take photographs of me, and the whole family made their way from the station towards the Adelphi Hotel. In the lounge, coffee was ordered and we all chatted excitedly. Alan Williams, the Beatles' first manager was there; Alan had written to me many times whilst I had been in prison. He and Bob Wooler had quite often written letters on one page. Their lines always cheered me up. They had always been good mates of mine. Then came an even bigger surprise. In walked Mr and Mrs Smith and my son Lee. I was overwhelmed. I hugged Lee and we both tried to smother our tears. Soon other people arrived, including the investigators who had worked with Mrs Smith in obtaining a voice sample of Terry Lyed. I shook so many hands vigorously and expressed my gratitude. I was so happy to be amongst all those who had always believed in me.

But then, by chance, someone passed a newspaper amongst us. It was the evening edition of the Liverpool Echo. My eyes scanned the large black lettering. I was headline news again. I read what they had led with:

CLUB OWNER RELEASED ON A TECHNICALITY

It then gave a résumé of my whole story. The only way they

would have obtained a story like that was via someone in the legal profession. These words were never used at my hearing. But they are words from a legal mouth. It is obvious that someone had contacted the paper from London and offered this inaccurate information to the press. Embarrassed at my release, I am sure they jumped in first to cover their own back. I was shocked. How could they do this? If I had been released on a technicality, surely I should have been re-arrested outside the court and charged again. I shook my head in despair. Why had they done this to me? My conviction had been quashed. I was an innocent man. My sons told me to take no notice; they insisted I just enjoy the day. They ordered one or two bottles of champagne and we toasted the future. My son Lawrence pulled me on one side, pressed some money into my hands. He told me he had arranged a hotel for me in Southport whilst I sorted things out. Gary told me he had been looking after some of my clothes and that they would all be ready when I wanted them. My sons did a wonderful job in helping me on to my feet again. They know how much I love them and how proud I am of them.

After a while the party started to break up with people making their way home. It had been a wonderful time and I began to feel encouraged for the future. When all the goodbyes had been said, Mr and Mrs Smith took Lee home with them on the understanding I would collect him next day. Firstly I had to rest and start planning a future for myself and Lee.

Since that extraordinary day when I returned to Liverpool, my life has been a daily struggle to survive. At the time of publication of this book, I am still on income support and I live in rented accommodation. Any attempt to go forward in business is scuppered by virtue of my recent history. In the eyes of the world I'm an ex-con; I have a police record. I was the man in the Hit Man case. I can't raise finance for business projects and on Merseyside, my whole family still suffer the stigma that has wrongfully been placed on the Armstrong name.

In January this year, 1995 when Channel 4 put out the *Cutting Edge* programme *Revenge*, once again I found myself the focus for more criminal association when at every turn, the blame was lain at my door, still I am portrayed as The Guilty Man. When I contacted the Channel 4 *Right to Reply* programme, they swiftly backed off. The truth it seems is too controversial. Yet they are quite happy to broadcast lies without the challenge of the truth. Their programme makers were either lazy or not interested in whether their programme was fact or fiction. Surely they should have researched this serious case before causing great personal suffering to me, my son Lee and all the Armstrong family?

I feel very bitter in the way some of the media have covered my case. No one was ever interested in listening to my side of the story. But then that is why this book has been written. My story had to be told. I want the world to know that I was always innocent, that I had no involvement whatsoever with the crime I was found guilty of committing.

Legal aid has provided funds for the action against the police. But it seems at every turn, I meet a brick wall. It has to be said that even now the legal profession is dragging its heels in helping me seek compensation for my wrongful imprisonment. In fact no-one in the legal profession has ever advised me that I only have 6 years in which to bring an action. This I learnt recently from a friend who had managed to bend the ear of a London barrister.

When first I attempted to take an action, three solicitors returned my documents stating they couldn't help me, this negative response often coming months after holding my documents. One legal acquaintance advised me to take it out of town. In other words, I would have no chance in the Liverpool area.

One barrister has said I have little hope of bringing a successful case against the police. I'm still awaiting advisement from another, a Q.C. no less. But somehow I feel rather pessimistic about the eventual success of such an action.

Recently a solicitor well- known for fighting good causes shook his head and said. "To be honest, I don't think you will be able to get a prosecution with this case."

I pointed out a number of things including how witnesses had not been called, the business of the edited tape. But he shook his head and gave it to me straight.

"You don't really have much of a chance of proving malice."

My whole case was dripping with malice but it seems proving it is a very different matter.

In the light of what has happened to me, I find this very unfair and disgracefully unjust. It seems this book is the only real hearing I will have; it is also the only way I can try and fight my way back.

The worst aspect of this whole story is the fact I still cannot gain access to David and Jonathan. Nor can Lee. Mr and Mrs Brown have quite categorically turned the idea down and have made every move to stop us.

In the past, my ex-wife has made ludicrous statements to the welfare officers to smear my name. My criminal history and those other lies now weigh heavily against me.

When I first came out of prison, I made several requests via the welfare to see my children. I was delayed at every turn. I then made a personal, unannounced visit to their offices on the Wirral. There I requested a meeting with the head man. When I was eventually invited into his office, he told me he was aware of my case; he also said he knew my history. I sat opposite him, and there on the wall was a photograph of him wearing a chain of office. My heart sank. In the past I had seen a photograph of Roy Brown wearing a chain of office very similar to the one this chap was wearing. Whilst I am aware of the good works some societies provide, I saw this chain as a link between this man and Roy Brown. I felt the chain was now being pulled tighter and that I was still tethered to my recent past. In dark corners there were those still telling lies. They had been hammered home and furnaced as strong as the shiny metal joints that had fired that chain together.

At my last request to see my children, the Lady Justice said,

"Prove your innocence and you can see your children."

211

In other words, I am still seen as a guilty man! It makes no odds to her that Lord Justice Steyn allowed my appeal and quashed my conviction.

I have not seen those two little boys for five years, nor has Lee. What is tragic is that a social worker told me that she had spoken to Jonathan and he had said,

"Yes, I would like to see my Daddy, and my big brother Lee."

Well son, one day you will.

ONE DAY, ONE FINE MORNING.

****

"There are two sorts of laws, those of absolute equity and universality, and the bizarre ones which owe their autonomy only to blindness or to the force of circumstance."

Diderot. *Oeuvres romanesques*

MY FINE BOYS

ONCE UPON A TIME
YOUR DADDY HELD YOU IN HIS ARMS
ONCE UPON A TIME
NOW LIVES IN MY HEART
I WAS NEVER GUILTY
OF THE LIES THEY TOLD THE WORLD
MY ONLY CRIME
WAS JUST MY LOVE FOR YOU

BAD THINGS CAN HAPPEN
BETWEEN A MAN AND WIFE
PROBLEMS AND WORRIES
ARE A PART OF LIFE
BUT YOU MY SONS ARE VICTIMS
OF A TERRIBLE MISTAKE
THEY PULLED YOU AWAY FROM ME
TO WATCH MY HEART BREAK

I AM SO MUCH OLDER
AND THE YEARS HAVE MADE ME WISE
BUT MY FOOLISH HEART
I NEVER COULD DISGUISE
STILL, THERE'S NO REGRET
NOT FOR A SINGLE DAY
YOU ARE THE FRUIT OF MY LOVE
THEY CAN'T TAKE THAT AWAY

ONE DAY, ONE FINE MORNING
I KNOW I'LL SEE MY BOYS
ONE DAY, AND IT'S COMING SOON
I'LL STAND BEFORE THEM
AND LOOK IN THEIR EYES
ONE DAY ONE FINE MORNING
I'LL KNOW THE JOY
OF MY FINE BOYS

Evelyn Doody 1994